RAISING A LOVING FAMILY

by
VIRGINIA SCOTT
GEORGE DOUB
PEGGY RUNNELS

Adams Media Corporation
Holbrook, Massachusetts

Published by
Adams Media Corporation
260 Center Street, Holbrook, MA 02343

ISBN: 1-58062-049-3

Printed in the United States of America.

J I H G F E D C B

Library of Congress Cataloging-in-Publication Data
Scott, Virginia.
Raising a loving family / Virginia Scott, George Doub, Peggy Runnels.
          p.   cm.
          ISBN 1-58062-049-3
    1. Family—United States. 2. Parents—United States—Life skills guides.
3. Child rearing—United States. 4. Love—United States. 5. Social values—
    United States. I. Doub, George. II. Runnels, Peggy. III. Title.
          HQ536.S396   1999
          646.7'8—dc21   99-12632
                                         CIP

This publication is designed to provide accurate and authoritative information
with regard to the subject matter covered. It is sold with the understanding that
the publisher is not engaged in rendering legal, accounting, or other professional
advice. If legal advice or other expert assistance is required, the services of a
competent professional person should be sought.
    —From a *Declaration of Principles* jointly adopted by a Committee of the
American Bar Association and a Committee of Publishers and Associations

Cover photo by Dan Bosler/Tony Stone Images.

This book is available at quantity discounts for bulk purchases.
For information, call 1-800-872-5627
(in Massachusetts, 781-767-8100).

Visit our home page at http://www.adamsmedia.com

TABLE OF CONTENTS

INTRODUCTION TO FAMILY WELLNESS

THERE IS DRAMATIC EVIDENCE THAT FAMILIES ARE FINDING IT INCREASINGLY DIFFICULT TO FULFILL THE EMOTIONAL AND DEVELOPMENTAL NEEDS OF THEIR MEMBERS. The exponential increase over the last two decades of divorce, teenage pregnancy, drug use, street crime, and school dropout rates points to an unprecedented need for skills and ways for families to cope with the many problems they face. A more subtle, yet alarming litany of problems experienced by families today includes a sense of isolation and alienation, a lack of ambition or motivation, a pervading pessimism about the future, and a preoccupation or obsession with escapist activities such as TV, video games, and mind-deadening music.

This steady disintegration of the family is one of the most poignant problems of our time. Everyone wants to have a good family life and be close and happy, but how? For all its many joys and rewards, the overwhelming experience of most families, even so-called "normal" families, is one of aggravation and confusion. The family is as much a source of negativity as it is for the warmth and support most of us want and need. Add to this phenomenon the increasingly more common complications of the step-family, single-parent family, adopted family, and widowed family, and it is certainly not surprising that many believe raising a healthy family is an elusive ideal.

For those who want something better and who are determined to do what is necessary to make their family more nurturing and supportive, a good place to begin is to recognize that healthy families take work, practice, and mastering skills we never learned. So many of us struggle with having grown up in a "dysfunctional family" ourselves, we have little confidence that we know how to create a healthy family life. As parents, about the only thing we have to go on is the example set for us when we ourselves were growing up. And since most of us receive no training in how to make relationships work or ever take a critical look at how we were raised, we all too often find ourselves simply repeating the mistakes of our parents rather than learning from them. It's no wonder that families need help.

Fortunately, not all of our family experiences were negative. Along with the mistakes of our parents, we also have as a model the things they did right. The majority of families are neither complete failures nor unqualified successes but something in the middle, with strengths in some areas and weaknesses in others.

What negative family trends fail to show is that some families, in the face of tragedy, painful separations, and many other adversities, still somehow manage to hold together strongly. Our conclusion is that these families succeed because they have the structure and skills to provide family members the stability and support to meet head-on many of the challenges of a difficult world.

The purpose of this book is to help you with the skills and ways of thinking that will allow both you and your family to draw the strength and determination needed to be successful, self-reliant individuals and to attain what we have come to call "Family Wellness." We don't offer a "cure-all" that guarantees family peace and love. Rather, we provide direction on how to develop the skills most commonly practiced by families who report "wellness."

We at Family Wellness Associates have a deep personal conviction that "Family Wellness" is not some elusive ideal attainable only after extensive and costly psychotherapy. On the contrary, we believe there is a relatively untapped wealth of skills and patterns common to healthy families that can be learned through simple instruction and practice. Since 1980, we've been in the business of promoting healthy families through Family Wellness Seminars. We've used compassion, humor, and respect through dialogue, drama, and group sharing to help over 200,000 families build on the skills they already have and learn some new ones.

This book combines our experiences as counselors, therapists, and seminar leaders with more than fifty years of research by marriage and family therapists working with families, searching for what works and what gets them into trouble. Again and again, family experts have observed the following characteristics in "well" families:

1. They don't rely on love alone, they develop skills.
2. A couple's good relationship sets the tone for the rest of the family.
3. The parents provide leadership and direction.
4. Family members can be their own person and still "belong" in the family.
5. Values are effectively communicated and modeled in the family's lifestyle.
6. The family adapts to change as necessary.
7. They can pull together to solve problems and achieve their goals.

These are the seven secrets of healthy and loving families—and this book will teach you the few key skills you need to develop. We will teach you, as we've taught thousands of others, how to create a good, solid foundation for your family and how to keep everyday problems from escalating into more serious ones. After reading this book, you and your family will have a much better chance at the happiness you've been trying so hard to achieve.

CHAPTER 1

LOVE IS NOT ENOUGH

YOUR MOST INFLUENTIAL SOURCE OF LEARNING ABOUT FAMILY LIFE IS YOUR FAMILY OF ORIGIN. Skills for living are passed on from one generation to the next in the course of everyday living. When you start a family of your own, you bring to this endeavor what you learned in childhood, plus any skills you've developed since. If the skills you have are effective, they will help you create a healthy family. But what if you, like many people, find that what you've learned is not enough? No, you're not doomed to an unhappy family life. You can change the course of your family history by learning new skills.

These skills are not difficult to identify or to master. Let's look at the skills that have been shown to be critical to healthy family life:

- Be your own person *and* get along with others
- Speak up
- Listen
- Cooperate
- Evaluate your "family skills"

BE YOUR OWN PERSON *AND* GET ALONG WITH OTHERS

Everyone has two basic psychological needs: the need to express his or her *self*; and the need to fit in with other people. Your sense of who you are and where you belong begins in your family. Healthy families nurture independence, confidence, and self-worth so that all family members can express their individuality. Family members are not dominated or prevented from being able to function away from their family. Healthy individuals love their families, but are still their own person. At the same time, healthy families provide a sense of belonging and connectedness for their members. They do this by providing a clear structure in which each member understands his or her role, and making opportunities to spend time together that build healthy rapport within the family. When life's frustrations, disappointments, and failed expectations seem overwhelming, the healthy family provides support, comfort, and consolation. Members of healthy families seldom feel alone or isolated. They have their family, and even if they don't always feel understood by their brothers, sisters, parents, or children, they at least know they are loved. This sense of connection is often enough to pull them through life's rougher moments.

Healthy individuals can more easily extend the sense of belonging and connectedness they feel at home to include their peers, students, and teachers at their school, members of their community or any others they choose to include in their lives. People who have developed these "connection" skills are more apt to be successful. Belonging to groups helps foster responsibility and stewardship as well as many other important values.

A family, then, should operate in ways that help its members be individuals and yet still connect with others. Unfortunately, these two needs often conflict. You are frequently torn between choices:

- Mom is exhausted and needs to sleep, yet her sick child requires care.
- Dad wants to spend time relaxing with his wife for the evening, but the tax deadline is approaching.
- Mom needs to work late to finish a project, but she wants to leave in time to go to her son's baseball game.

At any given moment, you must choose: Will you rest or nurse your sick child? Relax with your wife or do the taxes? Finish your work project or go to your son's game? Making a choice leaves you out of balance. One of your needs has been satisfied; the other has not.

To deal with these inevitable conflicts, each family member must learn to continually read the signals that they or others need either a little more room or a little more contact, and then adjust their actions accordingly. For example:

> My eight-year-old daughter was sick for three days and became very demanding: "Get my doll!" "I want some water!" "My blanket fell off!"
>
> I tried to be understanding. She'd been coughing and had a runny nose, and I knew she didn't feel well. At first, I tried joking with her and told her I was off duty. When that didn't help, I found myself getting sarcastic and calling her a "princess." Finally, I'd had it. When she whined and said I was being mean (after all I'd done), I hit the ceiling. I yelled, "I'll be your nurse, but not your slave!" and stomped out of the room. I sat in the kitchen and cried, feeling a mixture of relief and remorse. She was still sick for the next few days, but to my surprise, she was much easier to be with.

Family life is a series of adjustments and readjustments, as each of you figures out how to get enough contact to feel secure *and* enough elbow room to be yourself. To the extent that a family can meet these two goals for its members, it will be successful.

Three skills—**speaking up, listening,** and **cooperating**—are at the heart of the family's role in balancing these two psychological needs. In a healthy family, everyone is encouraged to express themselves and is rewarded for listening to others and cooperating to meet family needs.

SPEAK UP

In the past, families often gave one member (usually the father) the job of speaking for all of them. There was a single leader, one person "thinking" for the family. The rest of the family was supposed to learn to accept the leader's directions. Today, that "Whatever you say, dear" attitude doesn't work. Families are healthier when each member learns to **speak up.** Each individual is expected to participate in the day-to-day workings of the family and be ready to lead as their talents and needs require.

This might sound easy, but it's not. One of the most important parts of speaking up is telling other people what you want. It's easy to say what you *don't* want, but it takes more effort to figure out what you *do* want. When you haven't defined what you want, you're likely to come across as blaming others. Instead, try to figure out what you want and *say* it. For example:

> Mike comes home from playing football, tracks mud in the house, and flops down on the couch in his dirty clothes. To get the response she wants, his mother might say something like:
>
> "Mike, go change into clean clothes. Put your dirty clothes in the hamper and then sweep up the mud from the floor."

Instead of:

"Don't you know better than to come in here covered with mud? Look at the mess you've made!"

For some people, **speaking up** means changing their whole way of thinking and behaving, and that change can cause anxiety. For example:

Lisa was raised to "speak only when spoken to." She was quiet and hard to talk to. When people asked for her opinion, she hesitated and her husband, Neal, answered for her. Lisa resented Neal's talking for her, but instead of speaking up, she frequently complained about him to her friends. As she continued to talk about him, never telling him what she wanted to change, she found that she cared about him less and less. Meanwhile, Neal became less and less able to talk to her. They didn't feel close anymore.

When Lisa finally confronted Neal with how unhappy she was, it was like a dam had burst. But, with the truth out in the open, they could at least look at what to do about it. They decided to go for couples counseling. For the next six months, Lisa practiced saying what was on her mind. She was coached to think out loud, start conversations, and offer her opinion first before asking for Neal's. Neal was advised to speak less and listen more. He learned to paraphrase Lisa's ideas and build on them, wait longer for her to respond when he asked a question, and to be less critical. Over time, Lisa developed a willingness to speak up. She discovered that Neal, unlike her parents, sincerely valued her ideas.

Tips

- **Know what you want.** Take the time to think through family situations. You're used to being clear and specific in many areas of your life. You order specific items in a restaurant, and you tell a mechanic specifically what you want to have fixed on your auto. But when it comes to your family, being clear seems more difficult. There's a tendency to be vague and expect others to just know what you want and mean.

Try to identify specific issues and what you want to do about them. For example:

"When I come home from work, I'm often feeling tired and preoccupied. I need about half an hour of uninterrupted time to take a break and get settled in at home before we start discussing problems with the kids or the house."

- **Say what you want.** It's easy to say what you don't want, but it takes more effort to figure out what you *do* want instead. Try:

"I want to go out to dinner where we can both relax."
Instead of:
"I don't want to stay home and cook dinner every night."

- **Use "I" statements that are focused and concrete.** Say:
"I want us to go on a two-week vacation this year."
Instead of:
"We never do anything together."

Traps

It's also important to learn how to avoid behaviors that can destroy communication in families. For example:

- **Blaming or complaining**
"You never think about anyone but yourself."
- **Criticizing**
"Your timing is lousy. Can't you see I'm trying to get out the door to go to work?"

- **Expecting others to read your mind**

"If you don't know what I'm talking about, there's no point in telling you."

- **Finding excuses to let others do all the talking**

"She doesn't listen to me anyway."

LISTEN

Each family member must also **listen**. When you encourage others to speak and you take the time to listen, they feel visible. Their ideas matter. They're "somebody." When family members are listened to, heard, and understood, they're all more likely to speak up, contribute, and feel good about themselves and their experiences in the family.

To be able to really hear what someone else has to say, you have to make time, quiet your own mind, and focus on the other person. Don't assume that because you live together, you know what each other thinks. You don't. Be careful to keep your mind and your ears open, especially with your family.

"How was your day, Adam?" asked Marsha as she peeled potatoes for dinner. She soon realized she'd made a mistake. Adam launched into a story about his report on dinosaurs, and she was already impatient. She had a report of her own to give in class in an hour and dinner to get ready. "Adam, I really want to hear about your report, and I just realized that I'm too busy right now to do it. How about if the two of us go off to your room after my class tonight and talk about dinosaurs?" Later that evening, Marsha listened carefully as Adam told her about his dinosaur report.

You start listening by being quiet, nodding, making short responses with words like "uh huh" or "yes." Gradually, as you understand the message, say back (reflect) what you heard to make sure that what you heard is what the other person meant. The more accurate your reflection, the more satisfied the other person will be that you not only listened but also understood. For example:

> Johnny ran into the house after school crying, "I'm never going back to school! I hate Miss Kovac! She's so mean!"
> His mom turned to him and said, "You hate Miss Kovac and don't want to go back to school."

When people talk, they convey a range of feelings, such as happiness, sadness, confusion, and anger. They express those feelings with a particular energy or tone that is a vital part of the communication. To listen effectively, reflect back each of these three levels of what you hear—the words spoken, the feelings behind them, and the energy. If Johnny's mother speaks quietly as she says, "You're mad at Miss Kovac and don't want to go back to school," he may still feel unheard. For him to recognize that she understands the intensity of his message, she must capture some of his energy by raising her voice and getting closer to his tone.

Intense feelings are difficult to hear because people usually get anxious around them. Our tendency is to try to quickly "fix" the feelings. It's important that you resist trying to change others' feelings; it isn't possible to reflect their message back to them when you're trying to change their feelings. For example, Johnny's mother might have said, "You don't really hate Miss Kovac. In this family, we don't hate anyone." This response stops Johnny's self-expression, where good listening could open it up. A more effective response would be:

"You're upset and mad. You and Miss Kovac are on the outs, and you don't want to go back to school. You think she's mean."

Effective listening has nothing to do with agreeing or disagreeing, even though it's much easier to listen when you agree with what's being said. Johnny's mother is not saying she agrees that Miss Kovac is mean or that Johnny doesn't have to go back to school. To repeat his words is not to agree with him. She is saying, "I hear you." This will encourage Johnny to talk more and to clarify and work out his problem.

Another important listening skill is to avoid *traffic jams*. When others speak, their words often spark your own thoughts. When you respond automatically with your thoughts or feelings without waiting for the other person to complete theirs, you've created a traffic jam.

Curtis mentions to Joan, "I'm worried about the way things have been going at the office lately."

Joan responds, "Yeah, I know. I'm having some concerns about my job too. It's harder and harder to get motivated. It seems like I'm either bored or irritated most of the time."

This "You speak—I speak" style leads to traffic jams where no one is listening. Both people end up feeling frustrated because neither was heard. When family members learn to take turns, traffic jams are either avoided or quickly fixed. One person speaks at a time. Others are willing to put their ideas on hold and concentrate on the speaker, because they know they will be listened to when it's their turn to speak up.

Here's an example of how to avoid traffic jams:

"I'm worried about my work," says Curtis.

Joan thinks to herself, "That reminds me, I'm worried about my job right now too," but she holds that thought and keeps her attention on Curtis. "Tell me what's going on," she responds, switching to a listening mode.

"I'm not sure. I'm worried about John watching over my shoulder and giving me advice. I feel like he's not confident that I can do the job."

"You're concerned that he doesn't think you can do the work on your own."

"Yes, but I don't want to make a big deal out of it and make things worse."

Joan *reflects* Curtis's words: "You don't want to make things any worse."

"Yeah," says Curtis, "I'll just figure out a tactful way to tell him to lay off on the advice."

Joan's willingness to give Curtis her full attention helps him clarify his thoughts and express himself completely. Good listening encourages clear speaking. Having spoken and been heard, Curtis is now ready to listen. Joan senses that and speaks up.

"I'd like to talk with you about some of my problems at work too."

Get in the habit of taking turns speaking and listening. If each family member takes this small step, it will help build an overall pattern of communication and cooperation.

Tips

- **One person speaks at a time.** Put your ideas on hold and concentrate on the speaker. Start listening by being quiet, nodding your head, and saying short words like "uh huh" or "yes."
- **Gradually, say back (*reflect*) what you heard.** If you reflect back as you hear the message, you'll make sure you

understand what the other person is saying. The more accurate your reflection, the more satisfied the other person will be that you not only listened but also understood.

"I hate swimming lessons! I hate the coach! I quit!"

"You hate your swimming lessons and your coach, and you don't want to go back."

- **Reflect back all three levels of what you hear.** When people talk, they're communicating ideas and feelings, and they express those feelings with a particular energy or tone that gives context to the whole communication. For them to *know* you understand, you'll need to reflect back what they said and the feelings behind their words while matching their voice and tone.

Traps

- **Lecturing or preaching.** Intense feelings can be difficult to listen to because people usually get anxious around them. The tendency is to try to quickly "fix" or change the feelings. It's important that you resist trying to talk others out of their feelings. For example:

"You don't really hate your boss. It's just a job."

This kind of response usually shuts down self-expression. Good listening serves to open it up.

- **Creating traffic jams.** When others speak, their words often spark your own thoughts. If you don't wait for the other person to complete their thoughts or feelings, both people will end up feeling frustrated, because neither will be heard.

- **Interrupting.** Good communicators learn to take turns. This small change in family habits will help build cooperation between family members.

- **Not taking the other person's thoughts or feelings seriously.** For example, saying something like:

"I can't believe you're this upset about something so unimportant."

In order to feel comfortable expressing themselves, family members must feel like their thoughts and feelings are valued.

COOPERATE

Each family member has a powerful influence on the rest of the family. They are all bound together in a continuous chain of cause and effect. Whatever you do is going to affect other family members, and whatever they do affects you. How you respond to them affects how they respond to you. How you help them determines how they help you. You can see why it's so important that families develop good skills for cooperating.

Cooperation skills enable you to bring order to your communications, set common goals and work toward them, and solve problems. These skills also help keep differences of opinion from turning into problems. When people sense a conflict coming, they tend to get more insistent and less cooperative. When things get tense, that's when you really need to use your cooperative skills.

We all want to get our own way. The important lesson for families to learn is to take turns so that everyone gets their way some of the time. Parents need to make sure their kids learn the value of getting some part of what they want in exchange for letting others get their way some of the time.

Eleven-year-old Melissa came home all excited; "Mom, Dad, Laurel invited me to her house for a slumber party on my birthday! All my friends are going! I can't wait! This is going to be the best birthday ever!"

Unfortunately, Melissa's parents had already invited her grandparents to come for a surprise visit on her birthday. They had thought Melissa would be thrilled. She hadn't seen her grandparents in a long time, and they were flying in just for the occasion.

It's hard to be cooperative when what each wants seems so far apart. Melissa's parents could say, "We've already made plans. You can't go to your friend's house." But there is another way to address the problem, one that encourages cooperation from Melissa rather than just obedience. They can look for common ground:

> "You're a popular girl," said Melissa's mom. "You have an invitation from your friends and we've planned a surprise for you."
> "Really?"
> "Yeah. We weren't going to tell you, but now that you have this invitation, I think we all better put our heads together."

Melissa and her parents talk over their situation, keeping their focus on their common ground. No decisions have been made yet. Each person takes a turn speaking and listening. They avoid criticism by focusing on what they have in common. Good decisions flow more naturally from this cooperative style.

> "We want to celebrate your birthday with you, and we want you to have the best birthday ever."
> "I want to be with you, too, and be surprised, but I also really want to go to Laurel's slumber party."

Melissa's family decided to have her surprise party early so she could join her friends after dinner for the slumber party.

Tips

- **Each person takes turns speaking and listening.** For example:

"I feel like I'm on duty every day from 6:00 A.M. until 10:00 P.M. I work all day then come home and pick up after the kids and cook dinner. When I finally get them to bed, I'm exhausted and irritable. The next day, it starts all over again. I don't feel like I can keep this up much longer."

"Yeah, you're putting in long days at the office and coming home to more work. You really are doing a lot. It's too much, and you need a break."

"That's it. You know just what I mean."

"Yes, I do. I see you working all the time, and yet I feel the same way. It seems like there's always something that has to get done."

"I know you're under a lot of pressure too."

- **Express your intention to work together.** For example: "How can we work together on this?"
- **Look for common ground.** Stay focused on what you have in common. A cooperative approach that involves family members will lead naturally to better decisions. For example:

"It sounds like we both agree that something needs to be done but I'm not sure what we can do differently. Let's think this through and see if we can come up with something that will work better for all of us."

Traps

- **Cutting each other off.** Sometimes when others speak up and there doesn't seem to be a ready answer, you may feel like they're putting demands on you and become anxious.

"What do you expect me to do? I'm just as busy as you are."

- **Insisting on having things your way regardless of what's going on with others.** For example:

"You're the one who wanted to have another child. I told you this was how things would be. I'm not going to give up my weekends to help you with child care."

- **Acting helpless.**

"I just can't think about this. It's impossible."

EVALUATE YOUR "FAMILY SKILLS"

Families with sufficient skills are able to face troubles together as a family and resolve them. Even though they still get frustrated at times, they know how to ask for what they want, avoid blame, and expect to compromise. When they don't know what to do, they get help instead of resorting to withdrawal or coercion. Instead of meeting family needs, inadequate skills lead to more problems that require more effort to solve. Here are some common examples of inadequate skills:

- The person who speaks up too much is a **bully**.
- The one who listens too much is a **wimp**.
- The one who focuses too much on cooperation is a **nitpicker**.

If you see a little bit of yourself in one of these extremes and have a tendency to express yourself by either coming on too strong, nitpicking, or wimping out, then you need to learn some new skills.

Bullies

Bullies say too much about what's on their minds. When they try to express themselves, they go too far. They often throw their weight around in the name of free speech and intimidate others in the process. They're bossy rather than communicative, aggressive instead of assertive. Their goal becomes getting their own way, not cooperating to reach mutual decisions.

Many bullies take on too much responsibility. Since they don't negotiate well, they switch back and forth between doing more than they should and outbursts of righteous fury and withholding. They figure they do all the work so they're justified in overriding the needs of others.

Their spouses frequently retreat and become wimps:

> Craig blew up when he heard that Julie had bought a sofa. "What do you mean you bought it?"
>
> "We talked it over and agreed we could spend up to $700, and you said you didn't care what it looked like. So, today, I saw one that I thought would be fine, and it was within our budget. What should I do?"
>
> "I'll tell you what you can do," bellowed Craig, "you don't go off spending my money without asking me! You call them tomorrow and have it taken back."

As parents, people who tend to have a bullying style rule with an iron hand. They generally have too many rules and enforce them too rigidly. They may get compliance but their children learn to avoid them—either physically, emotionally, or both.

> At age twenty-five, Jaime wanted to go to electronics school. For years, his father had demanded that he live at home, work at his auto body shop, and help support the family. Jaime thought his other brothers should have to help with the finances too, but his father refused to discuss the matter. Three months ago, Jaime left home unannounced. His father hasn't spoken to him since.

Wimps

Wimps focus too much on the other person. They try too hard to fit in and please others, exaggerating the importance of what others say or think in relation to their own ideas. They keep their thoughts to themselves. Often wimps don't even know *what* they think because they're always looking to someone else for advice. They defer important decisions to others, believing that others somehow know more, and end up feeling neglected or demeaned. They lose themselves while taking pride in being adaptable. They assume a victimized, martyred posture and then feel justified in complaining and blaming others when things go wrong, and laying on guilt trips to get what they want. For example:

> "Larry wanted to go canoeing. He always has great ideas about things to do. As usual, I was scared. I said I would go but I couldn't row very well, so he would have to do most of the work. Everything started out okay. But then, we got too far out in the ocean, and the waves started pushing us out further and further. I couldn't keep up with the rowing, and he started yelling at me and telling me to do it right. We eventually got back to shore but ended up in a big fight. I shouldn't have gone. As usual, it wasn't fun for me. I don't know how I get stuck in these situations."

As parents, wimps tend to provide too little guidance for their kids. Often through helplessness or misinformation they may either neglect their children or focus too much on their role as nurturer and overprotect them. Their children eventually either take charge themselves or look for guidance wherever they can get it. They make decisions prematurely and take either too much or too little responsibility for their age.

> At age sixteen, David's mother can't get him to listen to anything she says. His mother, a single parent, hasn't been able to get David out of bed to get to school on time all year, and he's gotten further and further behind in his studies. He constantly complains about the teachers and other students, and his mother agrees with him in blaming others for the problems he's

having. Now, David has decided to drop out of school and says no one can make him go.

Nitpickers

Nitpickers tend to be too focused on details or "fairness." They insist that every issue be dealt with in a precise way, leaving no room for individual differences or for the unexpected. They rigorously and compulsively split everything in half; under no circumstances will they contribute more than "their" half on a given project. Issues are always either black or white, never gray. Any attempt by others to bring up complications is met with distrust. The spouse of a nitpicker typically withdraws into resentment.

Alice and Bob got married and moved into Alice's house. Alice insisted that every box of belongings that Bob brought into the house be opened carefully by both of them. She kept an account of everything, listing dates of purchase and estimated values. She planned to add up each of their contributions to determine whether things were "equal." Bob resented her focus on every little detail. It seemed to him like Alice somehow didn't trust him, and he started wondering if their marriage was a mistake.

Nitpicking parents tend to be *over-organizers*. They want to play a big part in their children's lives and won't stand back and let them learn by experience. In the name of helping they intrude, allowing their children too little room for self-expression. The children feel pressured and either rebel or give in.

Monique's twelve-year-old daughter, Julie, had been getting ready for her first dance, and Monique had spent the day hunting for just the right outfit for her. She even called the school and offered to chaperone and bring cookies. When Julie got home, Monique showed her the great dress she had bought for her.

Julie didn't want to wear a dress. "Jana and I decided to wear matching black blouses and jeans." Monique didn't like the idea of Julie wearing black, and said there was no way she would allow her to wear jeans to a dance. She wanted this to be a night Julie would always remember. "Put on the new dress. You'll love it. I spent four hours looking at dresses for you today." At that, Julie started crying and ran to her room.

Families can expect upsets and difficult times, but people with too few skills get off track more frequently and have a much harder time working things out. They will try and fail, until their frustration turns into despair, and individual behaviors that don't work lead to ongoing family problems. Learn to recognize frustration as a sign that something isn't working, and use your skills to do something different.

If necessary, seek out new skills. The skills you need to reduce upsets and achieve harmony are learned the same way you learn how to read, play the guitar, or use a computer—through study and practice. You can be happier and have a more fulfilling marriage and family life by adding new skills.

Think about how you respond most of the time. Then, think about how you tend to respond under stress. Do you have a tendency to:

- Speak up too much or too little?
- Listen too much or too little?
- Cooperate too much or too little?

Speaking up, listening, and **cooperating** are critical skills for strengthening your family life. To help you learn to reinforce these skills, we will show you how to apply them to different family members in a variety of situations throughout this book. By learning and using these skills, you can make your family life a source of strength, comfort, and fun. When you pass these skills on to new generations, they will become precious heirlooms—the secrets to a happy family life.

CHAPTER 2

PARENTS CAN COUNT ON EACH OTHER AS PARTNERS

MANY PEOPLE SPEND THEIR LIVES DREAMING ABOUT HAVING AN IDEAL RELATIONSHIP, RATHER THAN LEARNING WHAT IT TAKES TO MAKE LOVE WORK. It takes a special combination of commitment and skill. Your chances for success in any relationship are enhanced by your and your partner's ability to:

- **Commit yourself**
- **Be more your spouse's partner and less your parent's child**
- **Cooperate to meet each other's needs**
- **Practice fighting fair**
- **Learn to survive the "couple cycle"**

COMMIT YOURSELF

Being committed is important to couples because they need to be able to count on each other, and be willing to give support to each other, in a relationship that is permanent. Part of the bond that holds them together and assures their long-term success is their mutual commitment to making the relationship work. A common complaint we hear from couples sounds like this:

"I don't have problems in any of my other relationships, only with my partner."

In fact, you're not likely to have the same kinds of problems with other friends or in short-term relationships as you do with a life partner. Friends may stay together for a long time and go through lots of ups and downs, but learning to cooperate with a friend usually isn't complicated by the added passion and the daily routine of a couple's relationship. Casual relationships may include a lot of excitement and passion, but you don't have the daily contact with each other and the constant need to solve problems.

How Committed Should You Be?

Once you commit to a partner, you face a critical question which will persist throughout the relationship:

"Are we staying together because we want to or because we think we 'have to'?"

Some people lose themselves in the name of commitment. They want to preserve the passion and total togetherness of the "honeymoon" phase of the relationship. They get so overly connected that they stay together even when the relationship becomes harmful or dangerous. Their relationship becomes like a prison where they lose touch with themselves, their friends, and the outside world.

It is self-destructive to blindly stay in a relationship no matter what happens. On the other hand, you don't want to send your partner the signal that your emotional connection is so insignificant that you're ready to bail out at the first sign of trouble. Chronically "standing in the doorway" on the verge of leaving creates tension. Neither of you will ever really feel secure in the relationship.

Partners need reassurance that their partner will be there for them—not the extra tension and anxiety that can be caused by a partner's ambivalence. Healthy partners try to maintain a balance between their choice to be together and their use of agreements, values, and rules to hold them together through the normal ups and downs of relationships.

Another important part of your commitment is to make time to both be together and be separate. When partners don't spend enough time together, there's not enough closeness in the relationship. They go their separate ways so much that they convey the message to one another that they really don't need each other. At the other extreme, they may spend too much of their time together and not pursue their individual interests. When they're too close, partners sacrifice their individuality for security. Chances are they'll eventually lose their sense of being together out of choice, and will feel trapped. For example, how often have you heard:

"I'm only here because it's the right thing for the kids."

Or:

"I'm here because it's too much of a hassle to get a divorce."

You don't want to be glued together or drift too far apart. You want to balance being close with being more independent, having your own friends and doing your own thing. The two of you need to be together as a couple and still stand alone as individuals. The secret is to take care of your own needs and be dedicated to helping meet your partner's needs as well.

Tips

- **Make it your intention to stay together.** Couples who intend to stay together make a commitment to take good care of themselves and each other. Many problems arise naturally throughout the course of family living. When they do, your first line of defense is your intention to make your relationship work.

Expressing your intention to stay together signals your willingness to work your way past the inevitable problems:

"I want to make this relationship a good one, one that we both enjoy forever."

- **Keep a balance between being together as a couple and standing alone as individuals.** Couples need to spend time focusing on each other to keep their relationship close and strong. As individuals, it's important that they also pay attention to their own interests in order to maintain a strong sense of "self." Plan your time so that you have both enough time together and some time for yourself.

- **Think about what attracted you to your partner and what keeps you together.** It's easy to lose track of the positive aspects of your relationship amid the difficulties of working out your life together. Remind yourself about the things you admire about your partner. It will help you remember what makes the commitment worth the work.

Traps

- **Too much commitment.** This can foster uncritical, unhealthy connections and attitudes like:

"I'm just the kind of person who keeps commitments no matter what. I made my own bed now I'm going to have to lie in it."

- **Too little commitment.** The opposite end of the spectrum, which is characterized by an inability to commit. For example:

"Life is basically something you've got to do by yourself. You have to stand on your own two feet. You just can't tell about relationships. About 50 percent of marriages end up in divorce these days, so you don't want to get too settled in."

- **Too much togetherness.**

"Isn't she great? We've never been apart since we got married."

- **Too little togetherness.**

"My wife and I just don't like to do the same things. She knows I like to hang out with the guys and she's got her own friends."

- **Promoting insecurity.**

"Every time we have a disagreement, he threatens to leave."

BE MORE YOUR SPOUSE'S PARTNER AND LESS YOUR PARENTS' CHILD

One aspect of your commitment as a couple is your willingness to switch your primary loyalty from being your parents' child to being your spouse's partner. Typically, one of the tests of your fitness as a couple is whether you can let go of your parents enough that you don't organize your new life around them. Loyalty to each other is one of the most essential ingredients in your new partnership.

The degree to which you and your partner have developed adult-to-adult relationships with your parents has a serious influence on your ability to have an adult-to-adult relationship with each other. If you're used to being treated like a baby by your parents, you'll tend to bring that same style to your behavior with your spouse. If your parents always rescue you from financial jams, you'll expect your partner to do the same. Unfinished business from your childhood almost always carries over into your life as a couple. You must learn to behave as an adult with your parents in order to be able to behave as an equal with your partner.

Your parents can have either a positive or a negative influence on your relationship. You can make the difference by taking the lead and acting like an adult with them. For example, keeping your agreements with them, being responsible about paying back money you borrow, and resisting the temptation to dump all your worries on them. Your parents can help by holding you to your agreements, treating you more like a friend instead of always giving you advice, and letting you know when they feel like you're inviting them to step into your affairs.

If you call your parents every day and spend time with them even when your partner wants to do something else, you're probably over-involved with them. If you never see your parents because they drive you nuts you've likely cut them off too much or haven't figured out how to talk with them as an adult. Either of these approaches weakens your chances of having a good relationship as part of a couple.

Do Your Parents Support Your Relationship with Your Partner?

Complete the following scale to see whether your parents do or don't support your relationship as a couple. When you have completed the list, spend fifteen minutes reviewing it. Ask your partner to complete the list as well. Talk over both your answers and your partner's.

Respond on a scale of 1-5:

1 = definitely false
2 = often false
3 = neither true nor false
4 = usually true
5 = definitely true

____ 1. My parents are supportive of my choice of a partner.
____ 2. My parents respect my right to make decisions on my own.
____ 3. I am happy with the way my parents treat us as a couple.
____ 4. I am happy with the way my parents treat my partner.

___ 5. My parents expect me to care for them in ways and to an extent that I consider inappropriate.

___ 6. If faced with having to choose on some issue or circumstance, I am more often my spouse's partner than my parents' child.

___ 7. I can comfortably invite my parents into our home.

___ 8. I like the way my partner treats my parents.

___ 9. My mother keeps a good balance between being available to help me and expecting me to run my own life.

___ 10. My father keeps a good balance between being available to help me and expecting me to run my own life.

___ 11. I can count on my mother to say no to me if I ask too much of her.

___ 12. I can count on my father to say no to me if I ask too much of him.

___ 13. My mother makes no attempts to undermine my life with my spouse.

___ 14. My father makes no attempts to undermine my life with my spouse.

___ 15. My partner feels welcomed and respected by my family.

Now, if possible, ask each of your parents to complete this exercise. Compare their responses to yours. Do they see the situation the way you do?

Tips

• **Spend time with your family because you want to, not out of a sense of guilt or obligation.** When you do plan to be with your family, make sure it works for both you and your partner.

• **Support family traditions and cultivate new ones.** Your parents have their traditions, and you'll need to create some of your own. If you just go along with theirs, you'll resent it. If you refuse to participate in theirs, they'll resent it.

- **Talk honestly and directly about your needs—and your parents'—and then cooperate to work out a fair and balanced approach.** There will be times when you get pulled in one direction by your parents and in another by your partner. This is a common problem. You shouldn't have to push your parents away or be mean to your partner. You just need to speak up—and stay committed to working through the issues.

- **Tell your parents more about how you take care of yourself and less about how you get into jams.** You're an adult, and if you go to your parents telling them everything that's wrong, they get worried. Parents need to balance being available to help and expecting you to run your own life, and hearing about your abilities will help them learn to trust you to take care of yourself.

Traps

- **Depending on your partner to help free you from your parents.** No matter how well intentioned, your partner cannot rescue you from your parents. You have to be the one to negotiate an adult-to-adult relationship with them.

If your partner says:

"Why don't you stand up to your mother once in a while? Just tell her that you've got your own life now?"

You probably need to work on establishing a more adult-to-adult relationship with your parents.

- **Putting your parents in the middle of conflicts with your partner.** If you remain overly connected to your parents and run to them every time you and your spouse have a disagreement, they're not likely to be supportive of your relationship.

- **Allowing your parents to undermine your spouse.** If your parents are always criticizing your spouse, you need to speak up. Let them know that even though you appreciate their concerns, you're committed to your relationship. Expect your parents and your partner to treat each other with courtesy and respect.

- **Waiting for your parents to change so your relationship with them will be better.** You need to be able to talk with them about the things you want so that you can spend more satisfying time together. They may be stuck in their parental roles and not know how to treat you as an adult.

COOPERATE TO MEET EACH OTHER'S NEEDS

Living successfully with a partner means making the mental switch from being someone who operates alone to someone who operates with a teammate. You and your partner must be committed to the view that the only good deal is the deal that's good for both of you, and that each of you are responsible for making sure that you *both* get a good deal. If either gets a good deal at the other's expense, you both lose.

Healthy couples believe that both partners' needs have to be taken seriously. Being aware of and respecting each other's needs and trying to meet them is one of the most important ways you demonstrate your caring and concern for your partner's fulfillment and well-being. Most people fail by mind-reading—assuming they know what the other is feeling or thinking without asking—and then acting on what they think is important instead of finding out what's really most important to their partner. In couples who are having problems, one of the partners often believes that the other won't or can't take their needs seriously.

Agree to a Balance of Power

Generally, people relate to one another from three different positions. They take a position above, below, or beside each other. You are in the "above" position when you're taking care of, in charge of, responsible for, or taking the lead. When you're being taken care of or going along with another, you're in the "below" position. In the "beside" position, you're relating as equals—doing things together, cooperating, and sharing the good and the bad equally.

Where do you most commonly see yourself in your relationship, and where do you see your partner?

- **Above**: You make most of the important decisions; you find it difficult or unimportant to include your partner in decision-making; you sometimes feel unjustly criticized or put down for decisions you have made.
- **Beside**: You take responsibility for thinking out your position on most important family decisions and expect your partner to do the same. You talk over most decisions, say what you want, and expect to negotiate until both of you are satisfied.
- **Below**: You take pride in being adaptable. You let your partner make most of the important decisions believing somehow you don't have as many answers, your input isn't important, or you're not smart enough for your opinion to matter.

For your relationship as a couple to work, your main goal must be to stay "beside" each other. Generally, the best way for you to relate to your partner is equal to equal.

Still, there will be times when you need to take the lead. Other times, you'll need your partner to take on more responsibility. At any given time, it's all right for one of you to be doing a bit more and the other a bit less. Moving from taking responsibility, to letting someone else take charge, to being cooperative, is healthy for your relationship. What's most important is that in the overall scheme of things, you can count on one another for support and you both feel like you're getting a good deal. Remember, the only good deal is one that is a good deal for both of you.

Who Decides?

The process of deciding everyday things like when and how to sleep, eat, talk, have sex, visit friends, raise children, and spend money is a struggle for many couples. It's not so hard when you agree, but when you differ, your coping skills will be put to the test. It's all too easy to fall into a pattern where one of you routinely takes on too much of the decision-making, while the other takes on too little. This usually leads to resentment on both sides.

Consider each of the decisions that follow and write a letter beside each to indicate who makes that decision.[1]

A. Mainly me   B. Mainly my partner   C. Together

1. Where to live   ____
2. What job your partner takes   ____
3. What job I take   ____
4. Whether we have children   ____
5. How many children will we have   ____
6. Rules for disciplining children   ____
7. How much time we spend together   ____
8. How much time we spend as a family   ____
9. How much time we spend with separate friends   ____
10. How many hours my partner works   ____
11. How many hours I work   ____
12. How much money we need   ____
13. How to spend money   ____
14. When to have sex   ____
15. How to have sex   ____
16. Whether we practice a religion   ____
17. How much time spent with my family   ____
18. How much time spent with my partner's family   ____

---

[1] Adapted from: Stuart, Richard. *Helping Couples Change*. New York: Guilford Press, 1980.

19. When to do household chores   ____
20. Who will do what chores   ____
21. Where to go on vacation   ____

Totals
___ Mainly me (A's) ___ Mainly my partner (B's) ___ Together (C's)

Each of your scores should be similar. The higher your score on "mainly me," the more you're operating from the "above" position. If your partner is making all the decisions, you're operating too much from the "below" position. If your score is about equal in terms of who decides, it's likely you're operating more "beside" each other—cooperatively, which is the best way for couples to relate to meet each other's needs as equals.

Know What You Want
You need to know where you're going as an individual before you can know where you're going as a couple. Most people think they know what they want for themselves and from their relationship. But when they try to put it into words, they find themselves saying what they don't want, or offering vague ideas and feelings, not specific wants. They start talking before they've taken the time to clearly understand what they want.

If you're like most people, you'll react to an event or question that makes you feel uncomfortable or off-center before you've had a chance to think through the emotional components of your response or reaction. When you do, you realize that you don't know what you're acting on or where you're headed. It's like the statement in *Alice in Wonderland*, "It's very hard to get anywhere if you don't know where you're headed." It doesn't even matter where you go if you don't know where you want to go.

Say What You Want

You're used to saying what you want in many areas of your life. In a restaurant, you know how to order specific items. You can tell a mechanic specifically what needs fixing on your auto. But it often seems much more difficult to tell your partner what you want. Instead, you end up saying what you don't want, you're vague, or you find excuses to justify not **speaking up**:

"She doesn't listen to me anyway."

"It would hurt him to know I feel this way."

"If she wanted to know, she'd ask."

Saying what you want to your partner involves skills that can be learned and practiced. As we indicated earlier, your first step is to know what you want. Then use "I" statements—sentences that start with "I"—that are focused, concrete, and express what you want.

For example, say:

"I want us to talk about what our needs are in this relationship."

Instead of:

"The only person you ever think about is yourself."

Practice saying more of what you *do* want and less of what you *don't* want. Even though it's often easier to say what you don't want, you're more likely to get your spouse's cooperation by saying what you *do* want.

For example, say:

"I want to have more fun, relaxing time together."

Instead of:

"We never do anything together."

Feelings are especially hard to talk about, yet they strongly influence your behavior. Complete the following sentences by listing specific behaviors. Then, ask your partner to discuss your answers with you. This practice can help you get better at talking about your feelings.

1. When I'm feeling tired or troubled, what I want from you is:

   _____

2. When I'm concentrating on other things, what I want from you is:

   _____

3. Some of the things I'm willing to do when you're feeling tired or troubled are:

   _____

4. When you are concentrating on other things, I'm willing to:

   _____

Get What You Want

Once you've learned how to know and say what you want, getting it becomes much easier. You won't always get what you want, but you and your partner can learn ways to get along with one another so that you each get most of what you want and need. As we pointed out earlier, getting what you want is always built on the foundation that the best deal is one that's right for both of you.

When you try to get what you want, you will often find out that your partner also has things he or she wants. When you speak up, it will probably also trigger your partner's feelings— and a point of view on the issues you're raising that is different from yours. Don't let these potential conflicts discourage you from continuing to move toward what you want.

Tips

• **Take responsibility for identifying your own needs.** What are the most important aspects of a loving relationship from your point of view?

- **Say what you want, not what you don't want.** Think of things that are happening currently in your relationship that you don't want. Then, write down what you do want instead.

What I don't want: _____

What I do want instead: _____

- **Be prepared to negotiate.** You want to get your needs met, not "win" at your partner's expense. To win, both you and your partner must be mutually satisfied. To start these negotiations, you must let your partner know that you're flexible:

"I want to find out if we have any common ground on this—I'm not interested in fighting with you."

- **State how you can help.** Make suggestions as to what you will contribute to a potential compromise or deal, as in:

"Maybe if I start coming home from the office a little earlier and helping out with the kids, we can have more time for each other."

- **Make short term agreements.** This way you can test whether both partners are satisfied by the new arrangement—without having to worry about committing yourself to a plan that doesn't work for you. For example:

"We can put the kids to bed by 9:00, and go to bed ourselves by 10:00. Then we would still have an hour of alone time, so we'd go to bed more relaxed. Let's try it out for two weeks and see how it goes."

- **Appreciate the little changes along the way.** And make sure to voice your appreciation. Your partner will be more motivated to make the extra effort that make deals requires. For example, you could say:

"Thanks for taking these few minutes to talk with me. It helps me to know that you still care enough about me to want to work on this."

- **Let your partner know when you have what you want.** Knowing that you'll acknowledge their efforts and that you don't take their compromises for granted is another way to show them the value of cooperating with you. For example:

"I'm feeling much better about how things are going now, and I feel a lot better about us when we solve our problems."

Traps

- **Assuming your partner should just know what you want without your having to speak up.** Don't criticize your partner for not being a mind reader. You need to share your needs with your partner or run the risk of disappointment.

It would work better to say "The most special present I can imagine getting on my birthday is for you to say 'I love you.' It really makes my day!" instead of "Why should I have to tell you to say 'I love you' on my birthday? Can't you figure out that flowers aren't enough?"

- **Bullying.** The partner who gets stuck in the "above" position routinely takes on too much of the decision-making and often communicates with a patronizing tone that suggests, "I'm better than you. I take care of you because you can't do anything right." Bullies also frequently feel confused and controlled by their partner's unrelenting demands for care. They alternate between periods of doing more than their share and giving orders to their partner. This kind of pattern leads to resentment on both sides.

- **Wimping out.** If you're constantly "below," you're a wimp. You've let yourself be taken care of too much. Wimps often turn passive, and pretend they don't have any power. Their tone and posture imply, "You're better than I am; I'm not able; I'm being picked on." You're getting taken care of, but at the expense of your integrity and self-expression—and at the expense of your relationship.

- **Nitpicking.** Nitpickers take a good thing too far. While aiming for a balance of power, they expect the scales to be absolutely equal at all times. What's important for couples is that both you and your partner must get what you need over the long run. There will be times when you need to take the lead and other times when you'll need your partner to take on more responsibility. It's okay for your partner to get his or her way at times, as long as you get your way at other times. You need to reach an overall balance, but not necessarily a moment-to-moment equality.

• **Making demands instead of requests.** Your efforts to bring change or compromise into your relationship must include your partner as a willing participant. For example, a statement like:

"Our sex life is going to have to get better or else."

isn't likely to move you closer to a deal, even if your partner is as interested in the issue as you are.

PRACTICE FIGHTING FAIR

Inevitably, you and your partner are going to have differences of opinion, and frequently, there will be a lot of passionate feelings involved. Sometimes you'll have to risk starting a fight to work out your differences. If you avoid fights altogether, neither one of you will end up feeling good or successful because the minor issues that could have been settled by fighting will have accumulated into major problems.

The idea of fighting in a relationship usually conjures up bad images. You think of people yelling, storming out the door, or even hitting each other. This kind of fighting is only one extreme on a continuum of conflict between partners. This range goes all the way from passive withholding and quiet, resentful anger to loud, boisterous, violent anger. A lot of men show anger quickly, before they show other feelings. Women are more likely to become depressed or cry, or engage in guilt-producing behavior, which can be just as destructive and out of control as yelling.

You can't always agree on everything. A fight can also be a starting point for solving a problem, or motivation for making a change.

Optimally, a fight should leave each person with their self-respect and dignity when it's done. The successful fight ends with each of you feeling heard and an agreement that satisfies both of you.

Let Your Children See You Negotiate Differences

One of the most important roles that parents play is to model for their children how people should treat one another. Children need to see their parents work out their differences—especially serious ones. If they watch their parents go through the process of getting tense with each other, acknowledging each other's differences, and then resolving the issue again and again, without damaging their relationship, they'll learn how to speak up, listen, and negotiate differences in their own conflicts. If parents resort time and again to winning arguments and don't take the time to hear one another out and negotiate their differences, their children won't have a model for the conflict resolution skills they need.

Hot Spots

Most couples have "hot spots"—subjects or issues they have a hard time working out. Typical hot spots include money, sex, time, and sharing work. For example:

> "The yard hasn't been mowed in about four weeks now."
> "Big deal. If you want it mowed, just mow it."
> "That wasn't what we agreed to."
> "We didn't agree to anything. I said I like to do some gardening. So I do it when I can. Now you're trying to control when I do it."
> "That wasn't the agreement. The agreement was that you would do the gardening. That means doing it when it needs to be done, not just whenever you feel like it."
> "I'll do it."
> (Meanwhile, he's thinking to himself, "I do a lot around here. I wish I got more credit, instead of

reminders of one more job to do. I did agree to cut the grass, but just to avoid fighting.")

In this situation, the first speaker doesn't acknowledge her partner's resentment. Instead, she pretends that they both have a deal they can live with. She doesn't stop to listen to his side. After all, she thinks she's right. She believes they did agree that he was to do the gardening. He is mad, but doesn't **speak up** and tell her what he wants. He just complains and gives her nonverbal signals that he feels like he's being taken advantage of. When either partner gets upset, doesn't listen or speak up, or ignores his or her partner's emotions, a hot spot can develop.

It's also common to develop hot spots around problems you've already tried to fix unsuccessfully. Each time the problem comes up again, it feels like reopening an old wound. Faced with differences of opinion that seem irreconcilable, you or your partner may stop trying to cooperate and resort to threats, violence, withdrawal, sabotage, passive resistance, or helplessness. You can get stuck in debates about who is "right," withdraw sullenly, or threaten to leave.

Sometimes hot spots stem from painful experiences in the past, often things that happened to you before this relationship even started. Nonetheless, working with your partner to resolve difficult issues is an integral part of building a strong relationship. It's natural to want to avoid a hot spot—nobody really wants to deal with such difficult problems. Maybe you sense that these issues hide even bigger problems, and you're probably right. But if you try to work your way around a hot spot, it will keep coming up until you do face it. If your partner seems to be agitated and upset when certain subjects come up, you can't afford not to face them. Some helpful hints for approaching potential "hot spots" are:

- **Encourage your partner to talk about it.** For example, say:

"There seems to be more going on here than meets the eye. I want to discuss it with you. Are you up for this?"

It's crucial that you get your partner to agree to face the issue. If that doesn't work, it can help to see a therapist or get other outside help.

• **Look for the common ground—some aspects of the problem that you can discuss without tension, and that can open the door to a broader discussion.** This can help even if the only common ground you can find is that you're both willing to talk about how it affects you. For example:

"We see this issue differently, but at least we're talking, and we do agree that we want to figure out a better way to deal with it than we have now."

Maybe the hot spot in your relationship is sex. Often, one of you wants to have sex more often than the other. In fact, few couples are perfectly matched in terms of how often they want to have sex. Or, maybe one of you gets upset about money issues. These issues can be very difficult to deal with, but you can't ignore them. Unless you and your partner learn to put your needs into words—even in extremely sensitive areas—you'll be vulnerable to trying to read each other's minds, misinterpretation, and unnecessarily hurt feelings. To sustain a healthy relationship, partners need to be able to experiment—trying new ideas and testing possible agreements—until they find a deal that works for both of them. This requires that they both **speak up, listen,** and **cooperate.**

Tips

• **Make reaching a decision that you're both satisfied with your highest priority.** Keep in mind that until both of you are satisfied, the discussion is *not* over.

• **Choose a good time to talk.** Some people confront their partner as soon as he or she walks in the door with a challenge such as, "Why did you spend that much money?" This is not a good way to start a productive talk. Choose a time that works for both of you.

- **Stick to one subject at a time.** It's common that as soon as you say, "There's something I want," your partner will react with, "Well, there's something I want, too." We recommend that you anticipate this reaction, agree to try to resolve your issue first, and then make sure to go on to discuss what your partner wants.

- **Agree to stay with an issue until you reach a resolution.** That means that you can't stomp out. You can't threaten to get a divorce in the middle of arguing over who's going to do the dishes. You have to agree up front that you'll participate in the process until you reach an agreement.

- **Take a break when you get stuck.** Sometimes it's not a good idea to try to figure things out during a heavy, emotional exchange. When you get to a point where you can't listen or think straight any more, take a break, but agree on a time to get back to the discussion. Even if the other person is upset and doesn't agree with the idea of delaying the discussion, you can say "I understand you're upset, but I can't handle this right now. I'll be back to discuss it with you in two hours." You go on record that the discussion is not over, and maintain your commitment to resolving the problem. This makes it much easier for your partner to agree to come back later. So, make an appointment, and stick with it.

- **Stay cool.** Cruel words said in anger are hard to erase. You are responsible for managing your strong feelings. Stop talking before you blow up and say things you'll regret later.

Traps

- **Bringing up unpleasant past history.** Sometimes in the middle of a fight, you realize that you're fighting with a memory. For example, your partner might say,
  "The last time we went out you were late."

When you discover you're fighting about something from the past, stop. Get back to expressing what you want.

- **Getting in the way of outbursts.** Sometimes people start out mumbling and grumbling, and then escalate into yelling. Responding with inflammatory statements like: "Don't you yell at me!" or "How dare you talk to me this way?" is like getting in the way of a volcano. Just get out of the way. Chances are, the eruption will pass within a few minutes, and you'll be able to return to the discussion.

- **Taking your partner's outrage and turning it into one of your own.** It's easy to meet rudeness with rudeness, anger with anger, stubbornness with stubbornness, but this toe-to-toe style never works. Take that angry energy and refocus it in the direction of getting what you want.

- **Harboring resentments.** Feeling resentment is a signal that you need to search for underlying issues. If you're both honestly trying to resolve a situation and you still don't seem able to reach a mutually satisfying agreement, it's time to say to your partner, "There seems to be something more going on here." You both need to be detectives looking for clues that will help you discover what feelings or issues are really blocking a solution. Maybe, despite your efforts to be straightforward in your discussions, you really think that you're not supposed to talk about a sensitive issue, that your partner's too mean to care about what you want, or that he or she wouldn't understand your point of view. You have to put those thoughts and feelings into words. Both of you have to say what you want, listen, and encourage each other to express your points of view in enough detail until you really understand, and then negotiate a solution that works for both of you. Again, the basic skills you need are **speaking up, listening, and cooperating.**

- **Holding each other to things said in anger.** You need to agree that things said in anger are not going to be held over one another's head for the rest of your life. People do lose control and say things that, in a calmer moment, they would never say about their partner. This does not mean that you should accept chronic abuse, or that you should learn to like being told painful information. It just means that you need to be able to both make apologies and offer forgiveness for the occasional mistakes made during times of high passion.

• **Thinking that you cannot fight in front of your children.** Kids who never hear their parents fight may grow up and be petrified when someone raises their voice at them. Children know when their parents are angry and whether they see it or not, they know if their parents are fighting. It's okay to be loud and fight in front of them, but not to be insulting or in any way physically abusive. When kids see their parents fight fair and work out their differences, they're learning valuable lessons they can apply throughout their lives. On the other hand, if they see their parents out of control with anger, or never resolving their issues, then they are missing out on important lessons in family living.

SURVIVING THE COUPLES CYCLE

Typically, couples relationships follow a certain rhythm, in which the partners, at various times, switch their focus from "me" to "you" to "us." Generally, the relationship starts with relatively high intensity, which then varies—there are times when the partners don't feel as close to each other, and again times when there's great intensity and passion. Couples repeat these stages over and over. We call this pattern the *couples cycle*.

The Wow Stage

The first stage in the couples cycle is the Wow Stage. This is the honeymoon stage, a time when the partners feel completely together and in agreement. You may feel united, strong, and wonderfully out of control. It can be a magical time,

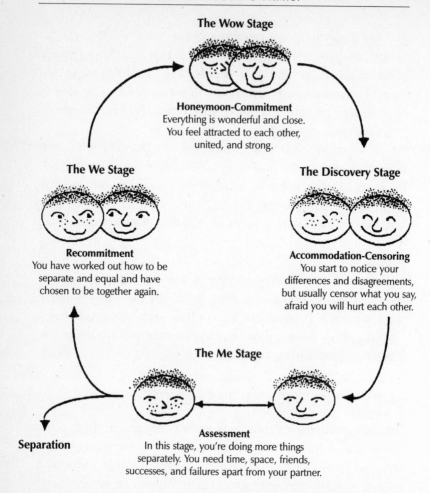

The Wow Stage

Honeymoon-Commitment
Everything is wonderful and close.
You feel attracted to each other,
united, and strong.

The We Stage

Recommitment
You have worked out how to be
separate and equal and have
chosen to be together again.

The Discovery Stage

Accommodation-Censoring
You start to notice your
differences and disagreements,
but usually censor what you say,
afraid you will hurt each other.

The Me Stage

Separation

Assessment
In this stage, you're doing more things
separately. You need time, space, friends,
successes, and failures apart from your partner.

whether you're noticing your physical attraction to one
another, going through your first experience of becoming parents together, or even successfully handling some crisis.

The challenge is to enjoy this magical stage. Some people
find it difficult to surrender to feelings that can be so fleeting
and so overwhelming. It takes a lot of courage for people to let
themselves feel vulnerable and committed to someone else.

The "wow" stage is characterized by the beautiful expressions of romantic love, such as:

"She's such a lovely woman."

"He's so gentle, caring, and strong. I never thought I could be this happy!"

"We do everything together."

"Time has no meaning when we're together."

"We're soul mates."

The Discovery Stage

In the Discovery Stage, you start to notice that your partner doesn't do everything the way you like or want it done, or you want to do things you think she or he wouldn't approve of. Perhaps the checkbook doesn't balance, or your partner sometimes talks too much. You may realize that you want to go places with other friends occasionally, that your partner's breath is not always perfect, that his or her ideas aren't all terrific. You often censor or hold back your thoughts or actions in this stage, afraid to "cause problems" or hurt each other. The challenge in this period is to figure out how to make room for your individual differences and still be together.

The key is to talk things over before resentment starts to build. It's equally important that you commit yourself to producing a criticism-free environment for those talks. You can say you're anxious, or you think differently, but you shouldn't say "You're wrong to think that way." Show respect for each other's individuality even when you disagree.

The Me Stage

During this stage, the partners start doing things separately. Everyone needs time, space, friends, successes, and failures apart from their partner. In fact, this separateness brings more vitality to the couple. It is a time to notice your individual strengths as well as your strengths as a couple.

The challenge of this stage is to be able to participate in independent activities without putting too much strain on your relationship. It's perfectly normal for you to be a little bit further away from each other at times. One of you may be traveling for work or taking a class. The other may be busy taking care of the house and children or working at another job.

But there are risks at this stage. If there isn't a foundation of trust, going in separate ways can jeopardize your relationship. If you both stay too wrapped up in your own lives, you will grow apart. This can even happen to couples who have lived together for fifteen or twenty years. When the children grow up and leave, the couple discovers that they don't know each other. They're strangers.

People are not machines and aren't synchronized together. Often, one of the partners moves into the Me Stage, while the other is still in the Discovery Stage. You may be feeling quite upset that your partner's off golfing or fishing on the weekend. Being out of sync can put a lot of strain on a relationship. It takes commitment and communication skills on each side to keep in touch when you've moved into different stages.

The We Stage

When you've made it through the first three stages, you almost always end up with a greater sense of commitment to yourself as an individual *and* to your relationship. You have found ways to live cooperatively *and* be separate and equal. You recognize the power of your team. You have chosen each other again. For most couples, this recommitment usually leads to the celebration of the Wow Stage again.

The challenge of the We Stage is to strike a balance between being an individual and being a couple. Couples need to plan time to be together. You need to spend time focusing on one another, committing and recommitting to your relationship to keep it viable. If you don't, it will go away. People say, "Gosh, we haven't spent any time together in three years. We've been so busy with other things, we haven't had much time for one another." They don't spend time together, yet they expect the relationship to flourish. Every couple struggles with this issue. Couples have to manage a balancing act between their individual needs and their relationship needs.

You'll go through this cycle again and again, and each time you have a chance to make choices. Just as you're both constantly developing as individuals, your relationship is unfolding as well. At every stage, a healthy relationship includes support for each other's individual differences and reaffirmation of your bond together. It helps to recognize the different stages of your relationship. Each time you go through them, you'll experience your relationship as more enduring.

Tips

- **Enjoy each other.** Learn how to let go enough to enjoy the Wow Stages in your relationship, knowing that they can be fleeting.

- **Talk things over before resentments start to build.** Couples often experience bitter times because, over the years, they haven't spoken up. They may have wanted to say something but didn't, telling themselves the time or place wasn't right.

- **Show respect for each other's individuality even when you disagree.** Learn to tolerate the normal tension that comes up when you see that the person you thought you loved is so different from you.

- **Keep a balance between being an individual and being a couple.** Hold on to your individual growth while still giving time to your relationship.

- **Make time to be together.** Spend time focusing on one another to keep your relationship alive. It doesn't happen by magic. Plan a date night at least once a week, especially if you have children, to make sure you have some time alone with each other to focus on your relationship.

Traps

- **Expecting to always be in sync with your partner.** People are not machines and don't always move forward at the same pace. It can be very stressful when your partner starts doing more things on his or her own while you're pulling to spend more time together.

- **Giving up things you enjoyed as individuals after becoming a couple.** Everyone has a basic need to "be their own person," and that requires having their own interests. This need may seem to go away in the early stages of your relationship, but can reappear in a sense of a loss of "self" as time goes on.

- **Not communicating enough.** You can get very angry and resentful toward each other in the Me Stage if you're each going your own way, but there isn't enough communication, or if you're miscommunicating by trying to guess what's on the other person's mind. If there isn't a foundation of communication and trust, going in separate ways can threaten your relationship.

- **Putting your relationship as a couple on hold once you have children.** It's difficult for couples to find time for each other away from their children but it's crucial to sustaining their relationship. Make it your goal to stay a couple, especially after having kids.

- **Waiting for vacations or holidays to spend time together.** This isn't enough time to maintain an open and trusting relationship. Even a few minutes together each day helps.

Being a couple is not easy. Still, the rewards are worth the effort. Those who succeed will establish a lifetime partnership with a friend, companion, lover, and playmate. Finding a comfortable fit with someone who knows you better than anyone else helps you to feel special and understood in a way that is unique to being part of a couple.

CHAPTER 3

PARENTS ARE IN CHARGE OF THE FAMILY

YOUR ULTIMATE JOB AS A PARENT IS TO RAISE CHILDREN WHO CAN THRIVE ON THEIR OWN. To mature into successful adults, kids need to have direction and control of their lives, feel good about themselves, and get along with other people. How they look at and interpret the world around them, the way they act, their values, and their sense of self-worth begin with their everyday experiences in the family. When the base of authority rests with parents, children learn to cope with life from a foundation of guidance. Once they are secure and grounded at home, they can safely reach out and experiment with life outside the family.

Kids are more likely to develop competent life skills when parents:

- **Stick together**
- **Make rules**
- **Define consequences**
- **Stay in charge**

STICK TOGETHER

Cooperating to provide direction and leadership for your family is not an easy job. Many adults are unsure of themselves as parents and have never had any training for the many challenges of raising children. Most people either tend to do things the way their parents did them—or just the opposite. It's not surprising that couples often have very different opinions about what works best with kids. For example:

"You know, Peter, I believe children are like little flowers. They have within them what it takes to grow, unfold, and bloom if parents don't inhibit them."

"I don't agree with you at all, Debbie. Children need to know what is expected of them every step of the way. This leaving them to grow on their own is a lot of nonsense. They need rules for every situation, or they'll run haywire."

"No, children need nourishment and encouragement. How else can they develop their creativity and individuality?"

"Individuality, baloney! If you stick with those permissive ideas, I'll bet the kids will walk all over you."

"I want the kids to see me as a friend, not a dictator."

"Not me. I want them to respect me and do what they're told. Otherwise, they'll probably turn into pot-heads or something worse."

"I want the kids to be able to talk to me and come to me when they need help."

"If they follow the rules I lay down, they won't get into any trouble."

Debbie doesn't believe in rules. She wants to play it by ear, focus on encouragement, and give her children lots of room for self-expression. Peter, on the other hand, believes in being strict and laying down the law to provide the direction he thinks kids need. As Peter sets limits, Debbie is likely to see him as being too hard on the kids and feel compelled to ease up. While she finds it easy to understand her child's point of view, Peter may see her as too lenient and begin to set more limits. Each of their behaviors triggers the opposite in the other until they find themselves on opposite ends of a see-saw, exaggerating their own behavior in an attempt to counteract each other's style.

This confuses children and leads them to take sides, often seeing one parent as the "good parent" and the other as the "bad parent." It teaches them to break rules or find their way around them—and to be sneaky and manipulative. The parent trying to provide leadership by making and enforcing rules will feel abandoned by a partner who sides with the child.

Tips

- **Try to develop a balance.** Create enough structure for your children to feel safe, secure, and loved while giving them enough freedom to express themselves and become their own person. Parents who make too few rules are too focused on encouraging and not enough on leading. Those who make too many rules are too focused on leading and not enough on encouraging. Your challenge is to find a healthy balance between the two approaches.

(This chapter focuses on helping you develop skill at leading and giving direction, while the next chapter emphasizes ways to encourage your child and promote his or her individuality.)

- **Negotiate your differences.** It is crucial that you and your partner work through your differences to give your kids a single, clear message about family issues. This requires making a commitment to work as a team, taking the time to talk, and offering compromises to find rules and consequences that both of you are willing to support. It isn't easy. You have to be willing to speak up to let your partner know what you're thinking—and that you want to be part of the decision-making process—, to listen to each other, and to cooperate to work out your differences. The benefits to your children will be enormous. They will know what's expected of them and they won't be as likely to try to play you off one another.

Here's a good example of a compromise in progress:

"Look, I think Rhonda is too young to date. But when I tell her 'no' and then you tell her 'yes' she's getting mixed signals. Let's figure this out together so I won't be getting mad at you for telling her 'yes' without talking it over with me, and she'll know we mean what we say."

• **Make rules you both believe in.** Parents find discipline issues get less complicated and anxiety-provoking when they learn to find a middle ground between their individual styles and make rules they both believe in. As partners, they feel more supported, and as parents, more confident when they establish rules and consequences they can both enforce. And it's more likely that their children will accept their direction if they speak with one voice. Their children will feel safer and more confident in following their parents' lead.

• **Stay on the parent team.** Family therapists believe that an out-of-control child is often "standing on the back"—or taking advantage of the support—of one of the parents. Parents need to be clearly identified as a team despite the pressures to "break ranks."

• **Make sure you both participate in disciplining.** Regardless of how easy it may seem to delegate this task to one of the parents, it's essential that both parents take part to make sure that your child gets the message that both of you support the discipline. For example, try saying something like:

"I'd like us both to sit down with Kim and talk about her consequences for cutting classes today."

Instead of:

"You'll have to handle her. You know she won't listen to anything I tell her."

• **Encourage and back each other up when enforcing a rule.** For example, Dave says to his wife in private:

"I know it's not easy telling Andrew that he can't have the car. I appreciate your doing that."

• **Support your joint decisions.** Both you and your partner need support as parents. You need to be able to bounce ideas off one another, and you both need reassurance that you're on track and doing a good job as parents. Husbands and wives who don't support each other don't get along very well. They often end up getting closer to the children than they are to each other.

• **Families work the best when primary connections are between people of the same generation.** That includes parents, grandparents, and kids. A mother and father's closest ties should be to each other. Grandma and grandpa's closest relationship should be with one another. And children should be closest to brothers and sisters.

Traps

• **Trying to work out all your differences in front of children.** Sometimes it's hard to be clear about what's right. You want your kids to love you. You worry that you're being too strict or too lenient. You think other parents may know better. All the while, your kids are pulling for one side to win—the side that agrees with them.

For example:

"Come on, Dad. Everyone else gets to stay out until midnight. Don't be so old-fashioned!"

"He is getting older, honey. Maybe we should let him stay out later."

"Look, Mom, all the other parents let their kids stay out that late."

It's normal; they just want what they want. If you and your partner are having a hard time coming to an agreement about what to do, it's a good time to take a parent-only break. Instead of trying to negotiate with both your partner and your child at the same time, get away from the kids.

Let your child know that you'll tell them the results of your discussion:

"Thank you for letting us know what you want and some of the reasons. We'll get back to you after dinner when we've talked it over and made our decision."

It will be easier to get together on the issue when you talk one-on-one.

• **Letting children have their way behind your partner's back.** For example:

Dad to child: "I told you not to go to the mall. Now you're grounded for the next three weeks."

Child to mother: "Mom, Dad is mean. He doesn't understand me. Why do I have to be grounded again? I never get to see my friends."

Mother to child: "Don't worry, you can go out. I'll talk to your Dad."

Or even worse: "You can go out. Just don't tell your Dad I let you."

• **Leaving all the decisions up to your partner.** Remember that your partner depends on you to support your parenting decisions. For example:

Maria's seven-year-old son, Andy, asks for candy, toys, and money every time they go shopping. She gives in more and more to the pressure of his constant requests and complaints, but wishes she hadn't. She asks Tony, her husband, what he thinks she should do. He is always too tired or too busy to get involved. Maria ends up making decisions alone and giving in to her son.

Maria loses because she doesn't get help from her husband and feels abandoned and alone. By not staying actively involved, Tony loses the chance to work with his wife and to develop a relationship with his son. Andy loses time and energy from his father and resents his mother. He gets his way because he's learned how to get his way around his mother. It's easier for kids to figure out how to manipulate the parent who is spending more time in charge.

Both mother and father can change this "dance." Maria can say to Tony, "I must get your help. I need to talk over what we're going to do about Andy wanting candy all the time." Tony can say, "I notice Andy always asks you for candy. I want to help out with this problem and figure out a way to get him eating healthy foods." Once Maria asks for Tony's involvement, she has to make room for him to get involved by not insisting that things be run her way. Both of them may need to modify their own position and embrace some of the other's position.

• **Getting stuck in the role of always being the disciplinarian.** If you're the one making all the rules and always being the disciplinarian, it will be hard for you and your kids to get close to one another. Both mother and father need to be able to work together well enough that they can step back and let the other parent take the lead at times.

• **Trying to be best friends with your kids.** Parents have needs that only peers can meet. They need their partners, advisors, and support system to be their peers. Their needs as adults cannot be met by children. If parents try to be best friends with their kids, they are going to feel chronically frustrated, and their children will be overwhelmed by their parents' problems—issues that are far beyond their years of experience to handle.

MAKE RULES

Rules are signs that point the way to what you believe and want for your children. They put your values into action by making it clear to your children what you expect of them. The result is predictable family behavior. Each person does their part and family members can count on one another. Rules are necessary to create order out of what would otherwise be an endless sequence of new choices, decisions, and behaviors—in other words, chaos. Rules point the way for children to live with others.

For example, common household rules include:

"Take your dishes to the sink when you finish eating."

"Share the candy with your brother."

"Be in the house by midnight after the dance."

"Have your homework done by 6:00 P.M."

"I want you to be drug and alcohol free."

Good rules don't guarantee your children's cooperation, but they increase your chances of getting it dramatically. Think through your rules carefully, so that you have a clear picture of the results you want the rules to achieve. The following steps will help you make good rules that are clear and specific—and stay focused on the results you want.

1. *Write down the situation as it exists now.*
2. *Decide on what result you want.*
3. *Formulate a rule that states the result you want.*

Present Situation	The Result I Want	Rule Needed
I have to nag Andy to get up for almost thirty minutes. He misses his bus at least once a week, and then I have to drive him to school.	I want Andy to get himself up, eat, and leave for school by 7:45 A.M.	Andy will set his own alarm. He will leave the house by 7:45 A.M.
Kelly comes home after midnight on weekends, and we argue.	I want Kelly in the house by 11 P.M. on weekends.	Kelly will be in by 11 P.M. on weekends, or she will stay at home the following weekend.

Explain the Rules

Take time to explain each rule and why you made it. Some children really don't understand why their parents have made certain rules. Let them know why you came up with the rule and check to make sure that they understand the rule and the consequences.

Here's a good way to handle this with your child:

1. **State the need and/or problem.**

"At least three days each week your homework doesn't get done. I want you to have your homework done daily, so you will do well in school."

2. **State the rule.**

"Your homework will be done by 7:00 P.M. each school day. You can make any phone calls only after you get your homework done."

3. **Check for understanding, then clarify.**

"I need to know if you understand what this rule means for you each day."

Your child might reply,

"What if I don't have any homework?"

"Then you can play with your friends or use the phone."

"What if I get it done at school?"

"That's fine, as long as the teachers say you're turning it in on time. We'll check with them at the end of each week to see how you're doing."

4. **Let them know the rewards or consequences.**

"If your homework is done on time, you may have phone privileges."

"Any homework missed during the week will be made up on weekends before you can watch any TV, make phone calls, or play with your friends."

5. **Post rules or charts that show time and work requirements.**

Reinforce the work they've done by posting a chart where your child can check off what was done and when. For example:

Homework	To Be Done By	Check
Spelling homework	7:00 P.M. daily	Tuesday, 6:30 P.M.
Reading report	Friday morning	Thursday, 3:30 P.M.

If your children have difficulty with their homework, sit with them as they do it. Even if you don't have all the answers, spending the time shows them that you value getting homework done.

Enlist Their Cooperation

You can also encourage your children to continue to do what you ask by giving them rewards.

Here's a simple process for encouraging them to cooperate:

1. List their jobs along with bonuses or rewards they receive for doing them on time.

"We've put the list of jobs we want done this week on the refrigerator. We'll check them off as they are done. If you finish them all, you'll receive your allowance for the week."

2. Reward the behavior you want.

Sonny, a seven-year-old, was having trouble in school. The teacher complained that he was talking to other children and disrupting the class. The teacher's solution was to move him to a seat by the door of the classroom. He continued to get up and talk to other kids. His parents met with the teacher to work with her to solve the problem. Together, they came up with a system. The teacher would send a "happy face" note home every day that Sonny behaved. The parents would collect the notes and Sonny could trade them in—five in a row equaled a goldfish; seven equaled getting back to his regular seat in class; fifteen equaled a movie. Within a month, Sonny had two goldfish, a movie, and was back in his seat.

With bigger problems like truancy, parents may need to spend more personal time and effort.

"You've been missing school even though I've driven you there each morning. I really want you to attend school so you'll have better opportunities in your life. For the next couple of days, I'll be going to school and sitting in class with you."

If their parents are willing to spend this kind of time dealing with the problem, most children will get the message that school is important. Besides, it's embarrassing to have their parents sitting in school with them.

Include Your Child in Making the Rules When Appropriate

Whenever possible, include your children in the process of developing rules and incorporate their ideas into the final form of the rule. Encourage them to think about the goals you want to accomplish and listen carefully as they offer suggestions. Children are more likely to cooperate with family rules when they've been encouraged to voice their opinions. This process takes patience, but your reward will be that you and your child will get a chance to talk together and understand each other better. You will still make the final decision.

Your discussions with your children about rules can be informal, or you may want to plan a family meeting.

In an informal talk, you can raise an issue when the moment seems right:

Lucy talks on the phone in the morning before school, after school right up to dinner time, and then after dinner until bedtime. She puts off her homework and spends little time with the rest of the family.

Dad talks to her informally by stopping her as she starts to make a call.

"Lucy, I'm worried about your spending so much time on the phone. Your homework isn't getting done, and I miss having a chance to talk to you. I know your friends are important to you. I'd like to hear your side of the story, so we can come up with some way to control your phone time."

"Dad, you don't understand about my friends. We're close. They even help me with my homework on the phone."

"You think I don't understand how important your friends are and how much they help. Well, they sound important to me, and I'm glad you have so many friends. Still, we need to figure out how to limit your phone time so your homework gets done, and so the rest of the family can use the phone. I'd like your ideas on how we can handle this."

"Okay, okay! Why not get "call waiting" so I could hand over the phone when a call comes for you or Mom? Or I could just talk after school until 5:00 P.M. and after dinner for two hours. I really need my friends. I promise I'll get my homework done."

"Lucy, you need to learn to balance the time you spend talking with your friends with getting your homework done. Starting now, you can use the phone after dinner for two hours—once I've checked your homework. If that works, we can talk about giving you more time. Call waiting sounds like it might be helpful too."

If you decide to have a family meeting to discuss rules:

1. **State the problem and the result you want.** Expect each family member to contribute their ideas on what the family's problems are and what they want to happen instead.

For example:

"I want your help in getting the laundry done so that each of you kids have clean clothes for school every day of the week. This has been bothering me, and I want to get it solved."

2. **Invite participation.**

"I'd like to know what you could do to help with this problem so that your clothes are ready for school, and it's less of a burden on me to get them cleaned."

3. **Get their ideas.** Expect all family members to participate in solving problems. Children are creative, so expect all sorts of solutions. They will contribute ideas that range from ridiculous to brilliant.

For example:

"Let me wear the same clothes for the week if I want to."

"I'll wash my own clothes."

It is important not to criticize their ideas. When you take the time to include them in developing rules, you encourage their cooperation and you reinforce the notion that children can help solve family problems. Many times they will come up with consequences for breaking the rules that are even more severe than the ones you would set:

"If I don't get my clothes washed and ready to wear for school, I'll have to wash the rest of the family's clothes for a week."

Whether you choose one of their solutions or not, your children have had the opportunity to think about the problem and contribute to the family. Whatever the result, your child has acted as a part of the family team.

Remember, not every rule lends itself to discussion. Nor does talking over rules mean that you are giving up your responsibility. You have to be in charge. You have the final say about what rules are needed, when they are negotiable, and what the consequences are.

All Rules vs. No Rules

Some families are run like a boot camp. We call these "Great Santini" families. They count on authority alone to protect and teach their children. Because they don't leave room for discussion, these parents run the risk of promoting opposition and rebellion instead of cooperation. Even well-meaning parents can fall into this trap. It takes skill to avoid creating the kind of resistance that can stop you from achieving your goals of teaching your children how to feel good about themselves, get along with others, and have direction and control of their lives. For example:

> Yolanda, a single parent, worries about protecting her thirteen-year-old daughter, Angie, from drugs and sex. She's afraid to talk to Angie about these topics because she might "give Angie ideas."

So, Yolanda made a list of rules that she thought would cover all the possibilities:

Rules for Angie

1. No friends allowed in the house unless an adult is present.
2. No makeup until you're sixteen years old.
3. Earrings have to be less than one inch in length.
4. Dresses must be below the knees.
5. Always wear a bra.
6. No friends over fifteen years old.
7. Return from all school dances by 11:00 P.M.
8. No dating until you're sixteen.
9. Be home after school by 4:00 P.M.
10. No reading "dirty books."
11. No talking dirty.
12. No movies rated PG-13 or worse.

While some of these rules were fine ways for Yolanda to put her values into action, making so many rules didn't put her in charge of her home. Yolanda got so tired of arguing over the rules that she felt exhausted and stopped enforcing them. Angie learned that her mother could be worn down by arguing—and that then she wouldn't follow through on the rules. For Angie, rules cannot take the place of her mother talking with her.

In families with too many rules, we see the following problems:

- The atmosphere is rigid and there's little spontaneity.
- Rules are often followed because of fear rather than out of an understanding that they will make family life better.

- The consequences for breaking rules are harsh and often physically abusive.
- Most of the parents' time with their children is spent enforcing rules.
- Parents and children don't talk to each other very much.
- One parent makes and enforces most of the rules and often feels lonely and misunderstood by the rest of the family.
- Children don't feel important.
- There is little room for self-expression.

At the other extreme, we call families with no rules "Flower Child" families. Parents who don't set rules don't give their children clear messages about what they want or expect from them. Sometimes, this happens because a parent wants to give their child the room for self-expression that the parents never had. Sometimes, the parents are just disorganized and don't really know how to think through their family's needs.

In some cases, the parents are so preoccupied with other problems that they neglect to provide structure for their kids. Whatever the reason, these families don't provide enough structure for their children to experience the sense of safety and belonging that families should provide.

Children don't have enough life experience to handle this much freedom. When discipline doesn't exist or is unpredictable, children don't know what they have to do to get their needs met, or how to measure up to their parents' expectations. They may even cause trouble to try to get attention and guidance from their parents.

When the going gets tough, many parents wimp out. They stop providing leadership out of fear of doing the wrong thing or confusion about what to do. If they continually neglect to provide leadership, grandparents, neighbors, or their own children will often take the lead.

"I told you to make Michael wear a coat or he'd catch a cold. You don't pay enough attention to that boy. When your father and I raised you, we made sure you were taken care of properly. Here, I'll handle him."

"Mom, why don't you make Scott clean up his room? It's a mess. All my friends' parents make their brothers clean up, and my friends don't have to baby-sit their little brother either. I'm not going to watch him today."

In families with too few rules, we see the following problems:

- Children have little respect for their parents.
- Children think they can always get their own way.
- There is very little sense of cooperation.
- Nobody is sure what's expected of them; They never know whether they're doing the right thing.
- Family members can't count on each other.
- Family members are expected to know what to do without being told and often feel guilty when they don't.

Some families try to make rules for everything. Others don't make enough rules. With too many rules, children don't learn to make good choices for themselves because so much has been dictated to them. Their parents run the risk of creating opposition and rebellion instead of willing cooperation. The problem with having too few rules is that it doesn't provide children with clear messages about what is expected of them. They need more guidance. They are children, and they don't know how to come up with their own rules or make good choices all the time. They don't have enough life experience to handle too much freedom.

Think about your family. Where do you fit on this scale?

All Rules <—1—2—3—4—5—6—7—8—9—10—> *No Rules*

Tips

- **Reach for a balance between having too much authority or too little.** That balance, or middle ground, is when you provide your child enough guidance to maintain predictability and order in the family, yet enough flexibility to allow for individual expression.

- **Be clear and specific.** Good rules spell out the results you want clearly and specifically. Rules that are too general confuse children and are harder to enforce. Be careful of euphemisms and generalizations, such as "act appropriately," or "I want you to be good." What does that mean? It's amazing how much better kids will hear you when you're clear and focused about what you want.

For example:

> Jim wants his fifteen-year-old son, Brian, home at a "reasonable time on school nights" so he can get enough rest and be ready for school the next day. So, Jim made the rule: "Be in at a reasonable time." Brian then came home after 11:00 P.M. several nights in a row. He argued with his father that eleven was a reasonable time. Jim changed his rule to be more specific, "Be home by ten o'clock on week nights."

- **Make rules that address what you want, not what you don't want.** Good rules say what you want instead of what you don't want. Positive rules are like signposts that direct children's attention and energy in the direction of what you want.

You want your teenager in by dark on week nights:

"I want you in by 8:00 P.M. on week nights."

You want your children to do their homework, before they are tired from playing:

"Your homework is to be done by 6:00 P.M. After it's done, you can play with your friends."

- **Use statements, not questions.** Make sure you state what you want instead of asking it as a question. If you ask children to do something, they may interpret this as though they have a choice.

  For example, say:

  "I want you to take out the garbage now."

  Instead of:

  "Will you take out the garbage?"

- **Be aware of how you say what you want.** Your voice tone, gestures, and expressions should convey the same message as the words you use. Rehearse your "I mean business" voice. Interestingly enough, kids almost always come around when they know their parents are serious. Unfortunately, parents usually don't reach this point until they've already told the kids to do something several times. By then, they're mad—and they sound mad. Sending the message that you're angry doesn't tell your child what to do. Practice using a tone that says, "Do it now!" without being or sounding angry.

- **Take the time to show them how.** Some children have no idea how to do the jobs you've given them. Show them how you want the job done. If you spend some time showing them exactly what you want done and how you want it done, even doing the chore with them at first, you'll probably save time in the long run.

  For example, you could say:

  "I want you to clean your room. I'll show you how. First, let's pick up all your dirty clothes and put them in the hamper. Then take all your toys and books and put them away. Now, let's make the bed so it looks straight like this. Okay, now I'll watch you do it."

  Instead of:

  "I thought I told you to clean your room."

  "I did clean it."

"It certainly doesn't look clean to me. I've told you time and again."

- **Show appreciation when you get the results you want.** Make sure you notice when your child follows your rule, and say "Thanks."

For example:

"I like the way you've been cleaning your room each day. Everything is picked up off the floor and put in its place. Thank you for doing such a good job."

Traps

- **Trying to mandate a good attitude.** If your son took out the garbage and grumbled, he still took out the garbage, didn't he? We know you'd like it even better if he didn't grumble, but you only punish yourself by listening to his grumbling. If you respond to it, you're inviting arguments and debates about the rules you're trying to enforce. Ignore the grumbling. It's natural for children—like the rest of us—to complain now and then.

- **Making rules about what you don't want.** Rules that say what you don't want point your children in the wrong direction. When you describe what you don't want, your children get a picture of what's wrong. They are more likely to hear your rules as challenges and feel drawn to react. This invites them to debate with you and often leads to confrontations and more punishments, instead of encouraging the behavior you want. When we ask children what some of their rules are at home, they immediately say:

"Don't put your elbows on the table."

"Don't talk back to me."

"Don't leave your dirty clothes lying around."

"Don't leave a mess in the kitchen."

"Don't leave lights on all over the house."

"Don't talk on the phone so long."

"Don't come home late."

Saying what you don't want focuses their attention on the very behavior you want to avoid!

• **Feeling pressured to make decisions on the spot.** It's much easier when you can get together with your partner and negotiate rules before bringing them up with the children, but you can't anticipate everything. There will often be times when you feel pressured to make an immediate decision. Remember, you don't have to decide instantly.

For example:

"Mom, my friends are all waiting outside now! Please let me go, just this one time."

"Tell your friends to wait five minutes while your Dad and I talk about this."

You can be more relaxed about discipline if you keep in mind that time is an invaluable tool. Step back and think through the situation until you find a solution both you and your partner can support.

MAKE CONSEQUENCES

Rules without consequences are not effective. Kids need to know that if they choose to break a rule, they'll pay a price. They need to learn to cooperate in preparation for their adult life. When your boss says "Do it," you don't say, "I'll do it later" and then not get it done at all. Kids are learning about power and control, and they need to know that they cannot push people around to get what they want. Kids need to test limits—to experience your "bottom line" for themselves. They need to be able to push against you—without your yielding.

Staying in charge means setting limits and following through on consequences when necessary. To do this, you must learn to step back from the emotional aspects of the situation, enforce your rules without being punitive, and learn to accept that your kids are not going to like you at times. Your goal is to work with them and teach them to cooperate rather than trying to force them to do what you want by blaming, scaring, or hurting them. Here are some of the best ways to set limits:

1. **Offer alternatives that help children manage their behavior.** For example:

"Since you want to color, here's a coloring book. You can color as much as you want but it has to be in this book, not on the walls or furniture."

2. **Limit their options.** Limit their choices in toys, time spent with friends, foods, where they can do their homework, or whether a radio, phone, TV, or window is available. For younger children, you may need to put some toys out of sight or limit those available for play.

3. **"Time-outs."** These can help children calm down or get their attention by taking time away from other interests.

4. **Separate them.** Put children in a separate quiet place or have them go to their room until they are more settled and able to play together or be around you.

5. **Assign tasks or work.** One way to develop thoughtfulness in children is to give them certain tasks when they break a rule. The tasks or work you give them should be based on the job that they didn't finish. These work consequences can also be used to make up for lost time on other projects. For example:

"Since you didn't clean your room by Friday, you will clean it and clean the bathroom today."

"You broke the window. Saturday, we will buy new glass with your allowance money, and you and I will put it in."

6. **Restrict or take away related privileges.** If they misuse the phone, you can restrict their phone usage. If they break curfew, you can set an earlier time. This kind of restriction of privileges can include use of the car, TV, phone, or taking away any allowance or earning that was directly linked to the rule that was broken.

7. **Ground them.** Keep them home from activities or social commitments. Remember, this is to let them know you are serious about the family's rules, not to give them a life sentence.

Tips

• **Keep in mind that the purpose of discipline is to teach, not to punish.**

• **Make the consequences age appropriate.** Make consequences for young children that don't last long and that they can understand—like time-outs and limiting their access to certain toys. For older children, think more along the lines of restrictions, tasks or work, and grounding.

• **Make the consequences fit the situation.** Most broken rules cost someone time, money, or energy, or they involve the child's abuse of some privilege or the rights of others. Natural consequences are best because they are tied directly to what was lost, abused, or violated. For example:

"Your clothes didn't get washed because they weren't in the laundry on time. You will now spend the next two hours washing your clothes."

• **Inform your child of each rule and the corresponding consequences.** For example:

"The rule is to that you have to get your homework done by 6:00 P.M. If it is not done by then, the consequence is that you lose your TV and phone privileges for the rest of that day."

Traps

• **Having no consequences at all.**

• **Making consequences that are too punitive.** For example:
"If your homework isn't done, you will be grounded for the next month."

• **Making consequences that are too complicated.** For example:

"You will be restricted from having friends over or from visiting them if you come home late, don't get your homework done, don't get yourself up for school, get poor grades, have a bad attitude, or don't help out around the house."

• **Trying to be loving at the same time you're giving a consequence.** When enforcing a consequence, you need to be able to separate your feelings about the discipline from your feelings for your kids. If you try to be both loving and enforce the rules, you risk confusing the child, and taking the impact out of the message you're trying to send. For example:

"I know you don't want to miss seeing your friends, but I'm only making you do this because I love you."

What kind of message does this send? This is not the time to act close and loving.

• **Coming up with consequences on the spot when you're angry.** More than likely, you'll be too upset to think clearly and come up with effective consequences when you're angry. Whenever possible, make a list of rules and consequences in advance so you can be firm when rules are broken without feeling so worked up that you can't think straight.

STAY IN CHARGE

Family therapists believe that one of the single most destructive things that can happen to a family is when parents surrender their decision-making role to their children. Children are not their parents' peers or equals. They don't have enough knowledge, experience, or understanding to make decisions on their own without parental guidance. They need their parents to be in charge.

This does not mean that parents have to be mean, or that it's okay for them to act like dictators. It does not mean they shouldn't allow children increasing amounts of freedom as they grow older and demonstrate responsible behavior. And, it doesn't mean that children can't say what's on their minds or try to negotiate with their parents. What it does mean is that, no matter how old your children are, you have the final say about rules and decisions while they are living at home. Whether you are a biological parent, stepparent, adoptive parent, or relative, if you have accepted the responsibility of raising children, you must have the right to have the final say.

Time and attention are a parent's greatest resources for staying in charge. All children, from infants through teenagers, want their parents to spend time with them. Everyone likes words of appreciation, honor for a job well done, or some other sign of approval. Children are happier when they feel important and appreciated.

Children get attention from you when you spend time with them and talk with them—whether the attention is negative or positive. Save your attention as a reward for good behavior. Think of it in terms of providing "units of attention."

Child's Behavior	What You Say	Units of Attention
Rhonda leaves her clothes on the floor.	"Pick up your clothes."	1
	"I told you to pick up your clothes."	1
	"You act like you were raised in a pigpen."	1
Rhonda says, "It's my room, why can't I keep it the way I want?"	"Don't talk back to me, young lady."	1

So far, Rhonda has received four units of attention for not following the rules. She may get even more if she argues cleverly. Better yet, she'll really rack up the units of attention if her mother gives up and cleans the room herself. Why reward Rhonda for having a dirty room? Remind her of the rule once, and walk away. Be prepared to enforce whatever consequence you've established. Save your words to reinforce her good behavior.

Spend as little time as possible on behaviors you don't want. The more time you spend repeating yourself, the less likely your child will obey.

"Are you up yet?"

"When are you going to get up?"

"I told you to get up and get ready for school!"

"Please get up or you'll be late."

This child needs less attention and more action, like an alarm clock and some consequences. When you enforce your rules, you're taking action. This is when you need to follow through with the consequences you've planned. Many children tell us that they would respect their parents more if they would follow through with their consequences.

For example:

Vince and Shirley have a sixteen-year-old son, Bill. They love Bill and encourage him to think for himself. They don't have rules about homework, dating, or using the car. They figure he can always come to them if he needs help. After all, he's a young man now.

Bill ends up flunking out of school, getting in a car accident, and stealing radios from cars. When his family meets with a counselor, Bill tells his parents he would respect them more if they had told him what to do and followed through with consequences.

Tips

- **Choose consequences you are willing and able to enforce.** A lot of parents lose their effectiveness by making threats about consequences that they either don't intend to carry through on or wouldn't be able to carry through if they tried.

- **Consistency is key.** Even though it may not be possible to be 100 percent consistent, it's critical that you demonstrate a pattern of consistency if you want to stay in charge of your household. Behavior therapists point out that parents unwittingly maintain the behaviors they're trying to eliminate by intermittently reinforcing them.

- **Respond quickly when a rule is broken.** The time to act is when the rule is broken, not later. If you fail to act quickly, your child may get the message that you're not serious about or are not going to enforce the rule.

- **Talk less, act more.** There is a time to talk over rules with your children, and there is a time for action. Once you know they understand, remind them once and be prepared to take action. Too often, parents find themselves reinforcing the very behaviors they want to change by talking too much while enforcing a rule.

Here are a few examples:

"This is the last time I'll tell you that your breakfast is ready."

"For the tenth time, No!"

"I'm tired of telling you to get ready for school."

Effective enforcement is short and often QUIET. The child lingers on getting to breakfast, you say nothing, and hunger is her consequence.

- **Expect resistance.** There will be some tense times when your kids will say, "I don't want to." It's normal for them to want to do only what they want to do. We all have things we don't want to do, and we learn to do them anyway. You just have to be clear about what you want. Let your children know if they follow the rules, they will be allowed privileges—and if they don't, there will be consequences.

Traps

- **Feeling guilty for having rules.** Your children are looking to you for guidance and direction, and it's your job as a parent to provide it.

- **Getting sidetracked.** Enforce one rule at a time. Don't get drawn into other issues. For example:

"Pick up your room now."

"But I haven't finished my homework."

"Pick up your room now." Don't get sidetracked into the homework issue.

- **Changing your mind or giving in.** This lets your child know that you aren't really serious about keeping the rule. For example:

"Oh well, if you're late for practice, I guess you don't have to take out the trash."

How often do you think the trash will be taken out in the future?

- **Commenting on personality instead of behavior.** Make sure your comments relate to a specific issue, instead of personal attacks like:

"Why are you always so lazy?"

- **Teasing, lecturing, debating, blaming, yelling, name-calling, and threatening.** Don't get caught up in bickering or arguing with your child. Remember, the simpler and clearer the connection between behavior and consequence, the more likely your child is to understand and follow your rules. Arguing with your child about what a rule means does not teach respect for family rules.

- **Laying on guilt trips.** Deal only with your child's behavior and the consequences. Don't bring up other issues, as in this example:

"You know how it upsets your mother when you and your brother fight. Now she's in bed with another migraine."

- **Getting physical with your children.** Most parents know they're striking a delicate balance when trying to discipline their kids. Having established rules and ready consequences will help you keep from escalating to anger or even violence.

TIPS FOR SINGLE PARENTS

Even though single parents carry an incredible burden, it is possible for them to raise a healthy family. Some single parents find it easier to parent alone, without the frustration of making and enforcing rules and working through disagreements with an unwilling or unskilled partner. However, anyone who parents without the benefit of the checks and balances that another adult can provide is especially vulnerable to ending up taking extreme approaches to parenting issues. Basically, all parents need someone to bounce their parenting and discipline ideas off of.

If you're a single parent, we believe you must find someone you can count on to listen to you and help you solve problems when you aren't sure what to do. Whether it is a relative, friend, neighbor, or teacher, it's important to have someone you trust who will be there for you when you need to talk over what you're doing with your child. If you're dating, you may want to involve that person in helping you parent, but only when you have developed an established, committed relationship.

While any parent can end up doing too much or too little for a child, single parents are even more likely to develop these issues. Many single parents think that their children have been short-changed by having only one parent and try to do too much for them. This doesn't give the child room to grow and develop, and it often doesn't leave the parent enough time and energy to pursue the support of outside adult friendships. On the other extreme, some single parents are just too tired and overwhelmed from working and being parents to take adequate care of themselves or their children.

Single parents need adult support. Who is yours?

TIPS FOR DIVORCED CO-PARENTS

Even after you and your spouse have decided that you cannot work together as partners and have divorced or separated, you still need to work as teammates to get the job of parenting done. The real danger is that you will continue to fight your battles through your children.

You don't have to like each other to work as a team. You don't even have to agree on specific rules. You do have to agree on some basic ground rules:

1. **Each parent makes and enforces the rules in their own home.**

2. **Each parent respects the right of the other parent to make the rules in his or her own home.**

3. **If you are concerned that a particular difference in rules or consequences is seriously hurting your child:**

a. Think through what you want.

"I want Johnny to get his homework done, no matter whose house he's in."

b. Contact the other parent, and invite him or her to solve the problem with you.

"I'm calling because I'd like to work with you on getting Johnny to get his homework done no matter which of us he is staying with."

c. Look for agreement rather than differences. For example:

"You think he's doing fine and we shouldn't interfere. He's a teenager now and should handle his own problems."

"We both want him to handle his problems and do a good job in school. I'm not sure you know that the teacher sent a note saying he hasn't handed in six assignments."

d. Remember that your goal is your child's best interest.

e. Thank the other parent for taking the time to work with you even if you don't reach an agreement. For example:

"Thanks for taking the time to hear me out on this homework business. We have different ideas about what to do, and I'm not sure what would work best. Let's think it over some more and talk about it again next week."

4. **Get outside help if you cannot resolve your problems and continue to be seriously concerned.**

TIPS FOR STEPFAMILIES

Remarried parents create a blend of two families, each with its own history and style. Working with a new teammate and co-parent requires special thoughtfulness and extra time. Both parents are used to handling problems their own way, and their children are used to getting directions from their own parent. Stepparents have to work out ways to blend their parenting styles, include their new partners, and handle the likely resistance of children.

Children in "blended families" often go through a phase of resentment. They don't want someone else trying to replace the missing parent. Infants and younger children may adapt more easily to a new parent than teens, who had more time with their biological parent and are at a stage in life where resistance is more likely. They may try to have their own parent discipline them by saying things like, "He doesn't like me," or "She treats her kids better than us."

Initially, the biological parent should maintain the role of disciplinarian and gradually include the new partner. Children need to have it explained that the new parent is not replacing their "real" parent, but as one of the adults in charge, he or she is sharing the responsibilities of parenting in the new family. The process of successfully blending families usually takes at least two years.

Children Participate in Family Life and Become Their Own Person

BEING LOVING AND SUPPORTIVE OF YOUR CHILDREN IS A VITAL PART OF PARENTING AND MUST COEXIST ALONG WITH YOUR LEADERSHIP ROLE. You have the power to affirm or negate your children's sense of themselves as individuals apart from you, as well as their sense of belonging and self-worth. They look up to you and see themselves reflected back. When you reflect back love, acknowledgment, approval, and confidence, they begin to see themselves as someone who belongs, and who is capable and worthwhile.

The keys to encouraging your children to be both part of the family and to pursue their own individuality are:

- **Make time for your children**
- **Involve your children in family life**

- **Learn how to draw out your children**
- **Encourage independence**

MAKE TIME FOR YOUR CHILDREN

It is important for each child to be able to count on uninterrupted time with each parent. The amount of time is not
as important as the predictability. You might plan to spend
some time with each child weekly or even every two weeks,
and then arrange some times when everyone is together.
The critical thing here is to schedule your family's time so
that you've planned time to spend together as a family, along
with one-on-one time between mother and father, mother
and each child, father and each child, and the children with
one another.

Your kids want and need your attention in order to discover
who they are and to feel important. By paying attention to the
unique person each child is, you confirm their individuality and
help them develop self-esteem.

For example:

"Watch me. Hey, Mom, I can ride my bike."

"Watch me go off the high dive, Dad!"

"Look what I made for you."

"I got an A in Math."

"I'm the fastest runner on the team."

"My teacher says I'm good at spelling."

Have you ever thought about what kids are trying to say
when they write graffiti on walls? Inscriptions like "T.L. Was
Here!" seem to say, "I exist," "I'm somebody," "Someone,
please notice me!"

Children are greatly influenced by their parents' percep-
tions of them. If parents show that they genuinely enjoy their
children and want to spend time with them, recognize them as
unique individuals, and appreciate their accomplishments,

children are much more likely to see themselves in a positive light as well as live up to their parents' expectations.

Play

Children and adults come at life from two different directions. Kids deal with life mainly through play and adults mainly through work. Playing with your kids can offer you some relief from household routines and an opportunity to reverse roles with your kids. When you play with your children, you can get out of your role of being a leader for a time. You're at a level where your kids can equal you or, in some cases, even surpass you.

What are some of the activities you participated in with the family you grew up in that stand out in your mind as good family times? Family picnics? Camping? Going to Grandma's house? Riding in the car? Traveling? Stories? Snacks? Snuggles?

What are some things you can do with your kids where you can act really silly or where you don't have to enforce rules? Take walks? Ride bikes together? Play make-believe? Dance together? Play outdoors in the leaves? Throw snowballs? Play games in the car while you're driving? Sing along?

Why do you think these turn out to be such pleasant memories? Could it be the amount of attention your children receive from you? Moments like this can become family treasures—as well as important stages in helping your children develop their role as an individual in the family.

If your children are different ages—say you have a six-year-old and a fourteen-year-old—you may not be able to do the same things with both children. The older one may want to go shopping while the little one wants to roller skate. You might want to take them out individually, or you may want to make arrangements with your friends to help each other out in doing special things with the kids. Often several people in the family want to do something, but one doesn't. Usually, you can find one thing you can all agree on, whether it's going to a movie or on a picnic.

Rituals

Recent studies have shown that families who share rituals together maintain closer relationships than those who don't. Routines and rituals help establish scheduled times that every family member can count on. Taking a few minutes together each evening for a story, game, or homework is very comforting for young children. Just before bedtime is a good time to talk with them. Weekly family meetings are a good place to discuss and plan activities. Whether it's having meals together, going to church, or attending family gatherings to celebrate birthdays and holidays, routines and rituals contribute to your family's sense of belonging and togetherness.

Mothers and Children

Mothers typically spend more time with their children than fathers. Many men and women explain this arrangement with the view that a man's role is to support the family financially, and a woman's role is to be responsible for the home and children. In these families, women carry on the traditional roles they were raised in and men carry on with theirs. These assumptions frequently endure even when both parents are working outside the home.

Women try very hard to meet all the demands of parenting. They don't consciously or purposely try to keep men out of the parenting routine, but many mothers, just by habit and training, feel that the children are theirs to deal with. Many men and women grew up in families where their father was never available. Frequently, it doesn't even occur to a mother to ask her husband for help. Or she may ask for help a few times, and if he doesn't do it well she gets discouraged and just takes care of the kids herself. She may grumble about it but she probably won't approach her husband saying, "We've got to change the way this works. It doesn't work for you, and it doesn't work for me."

Mothers and fathers have strikingly different views on this issue. They need to help each other learn to parent together. For example,

Father: "You're always home when our children get home from school. When I get home and go to say hello, they're busy doing their own thing and don't want to be bothered."

Mother: "They're used to coming to me for everything. I don't always know what to do either. I want them to go to you more. I feel burdened and want to get away sometimes but don't know how. I guess I end up thinking you don't want to be with them."

Father: "I don't know what to say or do with them, but I love them, and want to be a good dad. Maybe Saturday morning could be your time alone, and mine with the kids."

Fathers and Children

Even though studies show that fathers spend more time with their children today than in the past, many men still don't know what to do with their children. They are removed from their children's daily lives, and they really don't "know" their own children. Some fathers are called upon only when help is needed with discipline, and they don't make the time to offset their "tough guy" role by being loving and playful with their kids.

Too often, men think that because women give birth to children, they instinctively know better how to raise them. Men play an important role in raising children. Both boys and girls need their father's care and concern for them as well as his strength and discipline.

How Well Do You Know Your Children?

Now that women are more actively involved in careers outside the home, they are also beginning to feel more removed from their children's world. Both mothers and fathers should answer the following questions—for each of your children—to get a sense of how well you know them.

1. What is your child's favorite game?
2. What is the height of your child (within one inch)?
3. What is your child's weight?
4. What is the name of your child's closest friend?
5. What is your child's favorite sport?
6. What movie did your child last see (not on TV)?
7. What is your child's favorite main dish?
8. What is your child's favorite musical group or singer?
9. What is your child's favorite TV show?
10. What subject does your child like most in school?
11. When was the last time your child cleaned his/her room?
12. What pet would your child like most to have?
13. What does your child like to do after school?
14. What is your child's nickname among friends?
15. Which household chore does your child prefer to do?
16. When was the last time you went shopping with your child?
17. What was the last problem your child brought to you for help?
18. What was the last present your child gave you?
19. What was the last nice thing that your child did for you that really surprised you?
20. Name two qualities your child has that you're proud of.

Plan on spending as least a half hour of time just to be with each of your children during the coming week. This is especially important for fathers who want to learn more about what to do with their children. Start by just spending time with them and getting to know them better.

Tips

• **Think about and plan your free time.** The key word here is *plan*. The chances are if you don't plan specific activities, things just won't happen. In today's world, there are lots of demands that can take time away from your family life. Still, most people have anywhere from twenty to fifty hours of free time per week when they're not cooking, cleaning, working, sleeping, etc. How much one-on-one time do you spend with each of your children each week?

• **Plan activities with your children that are fun and include physical activity and touching.** Having fun and being physically active produce the energy and freedom to keep you and your family feeling good and strong.

• **Listen to the things your children want to do with you.** What are three things you do together that your kids really like? When was the last time you did them?

1. _____

2. _____

3. _____

• **Do some things with your kids that are fun for both of you, not just what they want to do.** What are three ways you like to play with your child? When was the last time you did each of these?

1. _____

2. _____

3. _____

- **Make sure you attend to your family rituals.** What are some of the routines or rituals that bring your family closer together?

Traps

- **Assuming that you spend enough time together because you sleep in the same house and eat your meals together.** This is one of the big mistakes that a lot of families make. The fact is time spent "around the house" is frequently not quality time. Living with your children isn't the same as having a good relationship with them.

When people fall in love, they find time to be together. They spend a lot of time focusing on each other. Similarly, parents need to plan times during which they will stop their other chores and activities and really focus on each other and on their children.

- **Talking about finding the time instead of just doing it.** This is a classic trap for over-burdened and over-scheduled parents. Have you ever said, "Someday let's...."?

- **Thinking that you're responsible for entertaining your children.** Your children will only expect you to entertain them if you encourage that expectation. There are going to be times when your children will feel bored. It's not your fault, and you don't have to fix it. Trust them to sort it out.

For example, try this response:

"Mom, I'm bored."

"Yeah. It isn't always easy to figure out what you are going to do next, is it?"

Instead of:

"I'm bored, Mom."

"Oh, listen, why don't you call Judy? Come on. I'll call her for you."

- **Having to win, enforce rules, or always be in charge while playing.** Remember, they're your children, not the competition. Let your kids play and see what you can learn from them, instead of always trying to "coach" them.

- **Trying to teach a lesson in everything you do with your child.** Sometimes the most important lesson a child can learn is that their parent just likes to spend time with them.
- **Spending all of your free time out in the community.** A lot of families get very involved in soccer, dance classes, music lessons, band practice, swimming lessons, tennis, scouts, etc. While it's important that kids participate in activities and learn new things, it's equally important that parents and children plan time together at home.

INVOLVE YOUR CHILDREN IN FAMILY LIFE

It is important for parents to remember to involve their children in two basic aspects of family life—work and play. Assigning your children chores that benefit the entire family both teaches them vital skills for living and gives them a chance to be genuinely appreciated for their contribution to family life. Planning fun times together helps families balance their responsibilities for earning a living, going to school, and doing household chores.

WORK	PLAY
Necessary	Necessary
Provides income	Feels good
Gets tasks done	Provides energy
Teaches responsibility	Allows positive contact
Builds good habits	Makes life enjoyable
Teaches organization	Teaches creative skills

Children like to be included in the routines of family life and often feel left out if they don't have their own jobs to do. In order to feel like a contributing member of the family, children need to have responsibilities that serve the family's needs, in addition to those things they do that only serve themselves. You may already be telling them to pick up their clothes and clean up their room. It's also important that you give them tasks that you'll genuinely appreciate them for, like washing the dishes so you don't have to do them. Give them assignments that really help you, not just to get your chores done but to involve them in things that make a difference in family life. Children can do many things that can make your life easier, and it helps them because they feel appreciated. Kids love to get compliments.

For example:

"That was terrific. I really appreciate your getting those dishes done without me having to say anything to you."

Tips

• **Expect your children to support each other's activities.** Younger children might go along to an older child's baseball game. They may not pay as much attention to the game, but they support the family by being there with you. And the older one might want to come to the first grader's school play. If you expect each family member to support each other, witness one another's successes, and be there for one another in times of difficulty, your family will develop more of a feeling of loyalty and togetherness.

• **Be playful when it comes to chores.** If you chase them around with the vacuum cleaner making monster noises, pretty soon the smaller kids will want to vacuum. Some parents put on music, sing, and dance around the house while doing housework with their kids. Learning to be playful with jobs can have magical results for both you and your children.

• **Let your kids learn to do things for themselves and for the family as a whole.** Sometimes it's difficult to step back and say, "Thank you very much for having taken care of the dishes," even though the child didn't do a very good job. It takes patience to be able to tolerate the time it takes for children to find their own way and to get better at doing things.

• **Show your appreciation.** Write a note to your child telling him or her in detail about one thing they did this week that you appreciate. For example:

"The lawn looks great, Teri, and all the weeds are gone. Good work!"

Traps

- **Expecting all work and no play.** A child's primary job is school. They put in a lot of class time and homework time, and they get tired too. Give them ways to contribute without overloading them. Keep a balance between having fun times together and getting work done.

- **Correcting your kids when they think they've done something good.** Your child may say something like, "I took out the garbage this week without you having to tell me." A good response is: "Yes, and it made me feel great when you did that." Instead of: "Yeah, I wish you'd do that all the time. Why should I have to tell you every time? You know it needs to be done."

- **Allowing all play and no work.** Some parents, especially those who had to work very hard when they were kids, try to protect their children from work. They tend to try to give their children everything and shield them from the difficult tasks of family life. Unfortunately, this doesn't make children feel invested in family life, nor does it make parents feel truly appreciative of them. If your children are doing things for the family and contributing to the overall work of the family, you're going to appreciate them more than if they just live off of your efforts.

- **Doing too many things for your children.** Some parents try so hard to be good parents that they take over every time their children complain about having trouble with a chore. While you may feel like you're helping, you're actually handicapping your children by teaching them that someone else will always be there to do the work for them. Children whose parents take on too much of the work tend to become self-centered, lazy, and unmotivated.

LEARN HOW TO DRAW OUT YOUR CHILDREN

Children have to think for themselves and express themselves in order to thrive. Parents can help by listening and encouraging their children to talk freely about what is important to them, even when you don't agree with what they're saying. You can invite your kids to open up to you by creating a safe family atmosphere where all family members are able to speak up with the certainty that they will be heard and respected rather than criticized or belittled.

One of the single most effective ways parents can get their kids to open up is to develop good listening skills. In Chapter 1, we talked about how you start listening by being quiet, nodding, and saying short words like "uh huh" or "yes" to let the speaker know that you're listening.

Gradually, as you understand their message, you can say back (reflect) what you heard, to make sure that what you heard is what the other person meant. The more accurate your reflection, the more satisfied the other person will be that you not only listened but also understood.

Reflect Back Their Ideas and Feelings

When children talk, they express more than just words and ideas. They also communicate feelings. Listen for feelings in your children's statements. For example:

"I don't have anything to do."   Bored

"Why isn't dinner ready?"   Impatient

"I hate that stupid math teacher."   Mad

"Look at the picture I drew."   Proud

"I get to go to grandma's house in two days!"   Excited

"I'm a better speller than Jimmy. I should have gotten
    the reward."   Jealous

Children feel heard and understood when someone listens and reflects back their feelings as well as their words. Respond to your children by reflecting back the feelings and ideas they've conveyed. Just concentrate on what they tell you and nothing more. When you add anything or try to assert your own opinions, it makes them feel that you've shifted the spotlight to yourself. Good listening occurs when you build on their voice without trying to provide solutions or answers.

For example, listen to the mom in this example reflect her daughter's message:

"Mom, can't you buy me some sneakers like Jill's?"

"You'd really like to have some sneakers like Jill's."

"Yeah, she's so lucky. Her parents are rich!"

"It's hard to see her get things you'd like to have."

"She has five pairs of sneakers, Mom."

"Wow, you sound surprised and excited."

"I think I'll count how many shoes our family has."

Sometimes it's difficult to get children to open up to you, especially if it concerns a touchy subject. Speaking up can feel risky, and they may need your permission so they know it's okay. You'll need to give them a clear message that you can tolerate the subject before they'll begin.

For example:

"How was your visit with your Dad today?"

"OK."

"Did you do anything interesting?"

"No."

As soon as you get two one-word answers, you'll know you're on the wrong track. Rather than trying to pry your child open like a clam, it is time to change your approach. Talking about yourself is one alternative. This does not mean that you can lay all your troubles on your child. It means that if you want your child to be open with you, you have to reciprocate.

When you open up first, your child is not the only one taking the risks.

Here's a good way to get started:

1. **Start with statements about something that is happening at the moment, or has happened recently, to you or your child.** Tell your child what you are thinking and feeling in a few short sentences.

"Sometimes when you get home from visits with your Dad, I get kind of edgy. I feel sad that your Dad and I couldn't get along and you have to go away to visit him."

2. **If your child starts to talk, listen and repeat back what you hear being said.**

"And sometimes you cry and say Dad's mean."

"Yeah, you notice when I'm upset and say mean things about your Dad."

3. **If your child doesn't offer any words, say something to encourage them like:**

"I'm wondering what you think about when I do that."

4. **Make sure you listen to what your children say even if it is uncomfortable for you and thank them for telling you what they were thinking.**

"Sometimes it makes me think I'm not supposed to love my Dad because maybe he is mean. Sometimes it makes me mad because I miss my Dad, and I want to be with him too."

"Thank you for telling me that. Sometimes I just get upset. It doesn't mean I don't want you to be with him. I want you to be with your Dad, and I do want you to love him."

Take Time to Understand

While it can seem tedious to keep drawing out your child's feelings, this is essential to encouraging their self-expression. This lets your child know that he or she has a voice in the world, and it helps parents to better understand what their children are saying.

For example, listen to this exchange between parent and child:

"Johnny thinks he's so smart."

"You think he thinks he's really smart."

"He always takes all the crayons."

"You don't like it when your brother takes all the crayons."

"Yeah. He's Mr. Smarty."

"You think he gets everything his way."

"Yeah. He shouldn't get to take all the crayons."

"You think it would be better if Johnny didn't always get the crayons."

"Well, yeah, because I like to have them too."

"You want to have the crayons sometimes and you think it's not right for Johnny to get them all the time."

Avoid Criticism and Directions

When children make negative statements, instead of criticizing or correcting them, keep looking for their underlying message. Stay with them even if you don't like what's being said, and remember mirroring their words back to them does not mean you agree with what they're saying. This is not a matter of agreement. You're simply reflecting back what they tell you, in order to encourage them to tell you more.

Here's another example of mirroring:

"I hate Mom. She made me go to my room."

"You hate Mom because you had to go to your room today."

"Yeah, she's so mean to me."

"You think your Mom is mean."

"Well, I don't like to have to stay in my room."

"Yeah, it's no fun having to go to your room, is it?"

Notice how important it is just to listen and encourage the child, instead of correcting her for "hating" or asking her what she did to deserve going to her room. You have to move out of your discipline mode and into a reassuring one that says it's okay for her to talk. This is not a good time to offer direction or criticism. It is a good time to be responsive to what she may be thinking so she will feel listened to, not shut off.

Power Struggles

Power struggles can create endless trouble. Kids sometimes throw huge tantrums to get what they want, and parents can get mired in their own arguments, or even give in, just to put a stop to the struggle.

For example, here's a classic struggle about food:

Child: "I don't like this food. I want a hamburger."

Mom (anxiously): "You have to eat what's in front of you."

Child: "I don't like these tomatoes in the spaghetti sauce."

Mom: "Tomatoes have a lot of vitamins. They're good for you."

Child: "Well, I don't like them. They taste all squishy in your mouth and I don't like them."

Dad: "Your grandmother raises tomatoes in her garden, you know."

(The child starts pushing the tomatoes off the side of the plate).

Mom: "Do you want to be sick? Is that what you want? If you won't eat the right things, you'll get sick."

Child: "I don't want to eat anything."

Dad: "You are going to eat that. You're going to sit here until you do. You're going to sit there and eat everything on your plate."

Child: "I hate this food. I'm not going to eat it."

(The child throws the plate down).

Dad: "I'm sick and tired of this. You do this constantly. You've ruined our whole meal, and you've made everybody unhappy."

Mom: "You've got to fix him something he'll want to eat."

Dad: "You baby him too much, he's gonna eat just exactly what we put here."

The best way to circumvent a power struggle is to try some reflective listening, and give the child room to say what he feels. Then he'll be more likely to accept what you want him to do.

To return to the example:

Child: "I hate tomatoes."

Mom: "Oh, you don't like tomatoes."

Child: "No, because they're all squishy in your mouth."

Mom: "You don't like things that are squishy. What kinds of things do you like?"

Child: "I like bread. I like this bread."

Mom: "Oh, you like the bread, huh?"

Child: "Yeah."

(Then he goes on eating—and usually eats the tomatoes too).

Eventually, the parents make their own decisions about what they're going to do but they've offered this child room to say what he feels. Parents can say, "You need to eat a bite of every food that we have." Or they can serve family style, and make a rule that children have to eat whatever they put on their plate. Do not focus your whole dinner on catering to children, or they'll keep upping their demands until you set limits. Two different aspects of the parent-child relationship come into play here: 1) parents need to stay in charge, and 2) parents must give their children room to express themselves.

Real Talk

"Real talk" occurs when parents get beyond lectures, sermons, and war stories, and children and parents can talk openly to one another. Confrontations are often good opportunities to switch to real talk.

1. **Start with reflective listening:**

"You're always telling me what to do," says fifteen-year-old John.

"You don't like being told what to do."

"No. You're always telling me what to do. I'm sick of it. I'll get my homework done. Just get off my back."

"You're saying you will get your homework done, and it makes you mad if I remind you."

"Yeah. Just leave me alone. I'll do it when I want to do it."

"Right. I hear you. You say you will do it and that my coming down on you just makes it hard for you."

"Yeah. You're always coming in here and telling me, 'Hurry up and do your homework.' I know I have to do my homework. I'll do it when I get to it."

"You will do your homework but you want to be the one to decide when to do it."

2. **Once you've taken the time to listen and hear your child's point of view, then you can add your opinion.** The mistake people make here is they add their opinion before letting children make their point. First, listen and reflect back what you've heard, then add your thoughts.

Here's an example of a parent shifting between reflecting and offering his opinion:

Opinion

"John, it makes me feel really good to hear you say you'll do your homework. The teacher sent home grade reports the other day and said that you haven't been handing in your homework in math or in English."

"That was a mistake. I just didn't get to it. I handed in my homework, and it didn't get put down in Mrs. Smith's class. Then in Mr. Jones's class, I thought we didn't have to have it until next week and they didn't give us the book until late. It's his problem."

Reflection

"So you're saying that you did hand in your homework in Mrs. Smith's class, but it didn't get recorded. In Mr. Jones's class, they handed out the books late, and you weren't clear about when the assignment was due."

"Yeah, I'll be able to get my grades back up."

Opinion

"I get concerned when I get these reports from school. I see that they're expecting things that are not being done. You want to do your homework and you want to do it yourself without my involvement. I want that too. I need to know that you'll handle this or I'll figure you're not able to take care of business without my help."

3. **Carry through to real talk.** Try to share your concerns in a way that makes it clear that you're speaking from the heart:

"I really want to help you, and sometimes I'm not sure what to do. On the one hand, I see that you're doing a good job growing up. Then when I see these parts of your main job of being a student aren't being taken care of, I think maybe I need to step in. I'm not always sure what to do in this phase where you're shifting from being a kid to a grownup."

It's very powerful for kids to hear you talking from your heart. When they don't give you eye contact, it doesn't mean they're disrespectful or not listening. It usually means this is a big deal for them and they're nervous.

"Don't worry about it. I'll take care of it."

"Well, it will be a lot easier for me not to come in to remind you if I see that you're taking care of it yourself."

"I'll talk to Mr. Jones tomorrow and hand in that other paper."

"Great."

So far he has not been in the disciplining mode. Then he switches to establish a rule for this particular situation:

"I do want you to bring a report back by next Friday showing that all of your homework is in for this week and that all the late assignments are in."

Again, this reinforces the notion that the parent takes the rules about homework seriously and is willing to enforce them.

Tips

• **Repeat what you hear your child saying to let her/him know you're listening.** Remember, listening is a skill that doesn't just come naturally. It takes time, patience, and practice.

• **Take time to understand your child's point of view.** Focus on your child's experience rather than your parenting experience. If you want them to learn to speak up and express their feelings, it's important that you stay in the listening mode.

• **Avoid criticism and directions.** Remain encouraging and noncritical even if you don't agree with what your child is saying. When children say something controversial or provocative, and you stay interested and let them take the position as far as they want to go, you send them the message that you're interested in having them develop their own thinking.

A lot of the far out positions that kids, especially teenagers, take are their way of sorting out their ideas. They're going through a testing process, testing out new ideas until they reach a point where they can get more concrete and focused about what they believe in.

There's no better way for you to help them reach that focus than talking it through with them. If each time they challenge your ideas, you say "Wait a minute, you don't really mean that. What you really mean is . . ." or you discount their ideas by saying, "Don't talk like that," or you try to preach to them, with, "Listen, let me explain," you are silencing your kid's voice. If you are always an expert or a critic, they'll realize that it isn't safe for them to try out their new ideas around you.

- **Turn everyday situations into opportunities to talk and listen with your child.** Practice talking with your child about situations you've gone through together. Talk about how you thought through the situation and what meaning it has for you, and invite your child to do the same. Make certain that the child can say whatever he or she thinks and feels and not be blamed or ridiculed.

Mom (after a near accident in a car): "I was really scared! I was sure that car was going to hit us and we'd get hurt. When I get scared like that, I get upset and yell."

Teenager: "Yeah."

Mom: "I wonder what you were going through, thinking your mother may have lost her mind."

Teenager: "Well, I was scared too because the car almost hit us, and you were yelling. I thought you were driving too fast and not looking."

Mom: "It's hard for me to hear that, but I think you're right. I've been preoccupied lately, and I get so used to driving that I don't look. Thanks for telling me that."

Teenager: "Are you sure you're okay? You're not mad at me for what I said?"

Mom: "Yes, I'm okay. I'm glad you're not afraid to tell me what you're thinking."

- **Talk from your heart.** As a leader, you must stand apart from your children. When you want to get closer, it's time to reveal more of yourself. Young children benefit from idealizing their parents. It helps them feel safe and protected. As your children get older, you'll need to change from a leadership style that is primarily authoritative to one that is more cooperative. By letting your kids in on your thoughts, feelings, and concerns, they get to see the "you" beyond the role of disciplinarian. If children can learn to think of their parents as real human beings, they're much more likely to open up to them about what's important in their lives.

Traps

- Lecturing or preaching.
- Interrupting.
- Correcting the way they speak.
- Not taking their thoughts or feelings seriously.
- Rushing to answer questions or solve problems without drawing out your child's ideas.

The problem with these traps is that they prevent your child from sharing his or her thoughts and feelings with you.

ENCOURAGE THEIR INDEPENDENCE

Your children's sense of self develops from their experiences both at home and out in the world and their chance to think about these experiences. Parents need to be like a mirror that says to their child, "I see you." The child whose parent says, "I see that you drew a purple line down the page," experiences his or her existence and importance through someone else's eyes. That reflection helps the child consolidate their sense of identity. Especially in the first five years of life, a child needs his or her parents to be an active, available presence who reflects the child back to himself/herself. When parents say things like, "You have a nose. I have a nose too"; or "I notice that you want to eat now. I want to eat in about ten minutes"; this indicates to the child primarily, "I see you," and secondarily, "I see some ways that we are different." This way children learn to experience themselves as individuals who exist separate from their parents. They begin to develop an image of "self."

The smoother you can make your child's path to self-discovery, the less they'll have to stifle their personality. In other words, they can be free to become the person they want to be rather than who others think they ought to be. If they have to accommodate their personality to yours or other's too much, they will develop poor self-identity or a lack of self-esteem. Give your children enough room to explore their interests or enthusiasms, even when those are different from yours, and pull them back only when it's necessary for their safety or because of family issues. They will then feel the freedom to focus on their "self" without being afraid of losing your love and acceptance. Children need to be able to move toward their own truths—without having to sacrifice too much of themselves to please others—in order to grow up and become healthy adults.

Now, suppose your teenage son is in a rock band, and you don't like the music they play. Your child's music doesn't fit—for you. Yet you're also aware that it does fit with his friends. Your son knows what is contemporary for him. He knows he needs to make his own friends, and that he has found a way to be popular with them. This is highly valuable for him. What do you do? Do you encourage his passion or insist that he play a different kind of music?

You have your own values. When your children don't follow those values, you have to make a decision. How much individual expression will you allow, and how much will you insist that your child conform to your values?

This is a struggle every parent has to deal with. You have the responsibility for leadership in your family. And you have to continue to advocate what you believe in. As a parent, you must make your own decision, knowing that you want to exercise your leadership, but you also want to promote your child's freedom. Your kids are trying to grow up to be men and women. The more they have to oppose you to be grownup, rather than just be different from you, the more likely it is that you will end up far apart. Do your best to hear your children express different opinions without blaming them. Take charge if their expression interferes with your safety or dignity—or with theirs.

How much will you control, and how much will you give your children freedom to express themselves? We cannot tell you where that line is, but we encourage you to decide with the awareness that there's a price to pay on either side. Teenagers developmentally need to hear from their parents that it's okay for them to have their own mind. They're afraid that their "self" is dominated by their parents', and they need a high degree of reassurance that they are their own person.

How do you know when your approach isn't working? Lying, sneaking around, and power struggles usually indicate that you haven't left your children enough room for self-expression. They'll still express themselves, but they'll do it indirectly. You reduce your chances of having these kinds of problems if you give them plenty of room to express their feelings, even if you disagree. If you find you're in constant disagreement with your children, maybe you're being too rigid and need to give them more room to make their own choices. This is the basis for their self-esteem.

Promote Self-Esteem

You not only want your children to develop their self-image, you want that self-image to be positive. Self-esteem means that you have a positive self-image and feel good about yourself. In developmental terms, self-esteem is a highly precious commodity. When children feel good about themselves, their experience of the world around them and their ability to learn new ideas and important skills for living is greatly enhanced. When they develop a sense of being connected to or belonging at home with their parents, they aren't as worried about abandonment. Their sense of belonging helps them feel secure enough to venture out and become their own person—and to develop confidence and competence. This is the basis for their self-esteem.

Self-esteem is not just desirable; it is a fundamental psychological need. You can help build your children's developing sense of self by letting them know you appreciate their abilities and by encouraging their interests. Gradually, your focus on their abilities will be incorporated into the child's self-image.

Many people believe that all children need to develop good self-esteem is lots of attention, love, and positive feedback. Certainly these are crucial, but they're not enough. Children also need to develop competence and confidence.

Self-esteem is only possible when you believe you can do what you need to do to get by in this world, you can get along with and fit in with others, and you are a good person. People who feel weak and ineffective do not have self-esteem regardless of how much other people tell them how terrific they are. People who are so lacking in social skills or so self-centered they never learn how to get along with others don't find the relationships they need and want or have a sense of belonging. And, those who don't believe they are a good person cannot feel like they are worthwhile.

Tips

- **Be encouraging, noncritical, and consistent.** Maintaining a noncritical approach says that you'll allow your kids to have their own minds.

- **Keep in mind that self-esteem begins with "self."** To become competent and confident, your child has to develop a sense of "self."

- **Teach your children to think for themselves.** If your children know what you believe, trust them to experiment while finding out what they believe. If you try to talk them out of their opinions, all you accomplish is to talk them further into them.

- **Support your child in getting good at things.** Kids need to have their own interests and develop their own skills to feel good about themselves. This will build their self-confidence, give them more direction and control of their life, and make them less likely to end up as "followers." Encourage your children to get good at things they're interested in by noticing what they like to do, planning time for and taking them to activities, building on their strengths, and not competing with them.

- **Take some risks.** Start by taking small risks. Give your child a small amount of freedom beyond what he or she has now. For example, let your daughter stay out until 9:00 one night. Watch the results. If she comes home on time, let her stay out until 9:00 another time. After three or four times, if she gets home on time, gets up and goes to school the next day, and comes home and does her homework, then you might change your rule and allow her to stay out until 9:00 routinely. The point is to give your child some freedom and then watch for the results. Gradually giving room to your child by taking small risks will help you become more comfortable taking bigger ones.

- **Accept your differences.** Part of what makes each child a unique individual is how they're different from one another and different from you. Promote their individuality by learning to tolerate their being different from you. Notice what makes each of your children special rather than comparing or criticizing them.

Traps

- **Expecting to have a clear sense of what your children should be doing at a particular age.** You find out what your children are capable of by trying and testing new things, not by a simple rule or standard.

- **Trying to protect your children from growing up.** It's hard to watch your children's growing pains. Sometimes they fail, friendships break up, other children tell your children's secrets or hurt their feelings. This is all part of children growing up and learning to fend for themselves. You need to be there to listen to and support them, but you can't take away the pain of growing up. The goal of parenting is paradoxical—to provide enough closeness and encouragement so your children feel secure and loved and enough distance for them to be able to learn and do things on their own.

- **Focusing on who your children are not, instead of who they are.** "You're not doing that right," "You're talking too fast," "Why can't you sit quietly like your sister?" all focus children on who they are not, instead of who they are. Ultimately, this leads children to develop a poor self-image. All children want their parents to be pleased with them. The best way for parents to work with their children is to actively look for what their children do that is acceptable, and make those behaviors the basis of most of their contact. When a child behaves in a way that is not acceptable, the parent should point in the direction of the behavior wanted, assign consequences if needed, and spend minimal time on the problem behavior. This way, children learn to expect to have their good qualities pointed out, and to have negative behavior handled with respect and redirection.

- **Hovering.** Some parents attempt to promote their own security at the expense of their child's independence. Be careful not to ask your children to take care of you when they're trying to step away from you. If you worry about your kids, especially teenagers, to a point where your questioning goes beyond information gathering, you may be focusing on your worries as a way to delay taking risks. "Where are you going? What are you going to be doing? Who are these guys you're going to be with? Do you think they have good character? Are you sure you're going to be okay?" This starts to sound more like requests for help with your own anxiety. The message you're sending them is: "Calm me down, so I can free you up."

- **Opening up too much distance.** Parents who show too little concern don't offer their children enough protection or security, and their children are left alone with their struggles. When kids can't get anyone to notice what they're good at, they stop trying to express themselves. They may seem "shy," "withdrawn," or "bored." Others may try to get your attention by "acting out."

CHAPTER 5

PARENTS MODEL THEIR VALUES

KIDS LEARN VALUES THE SAME WAY THEY LEARN OTHER THINGS—by watching, imitating, and thinking about what they've seen and experienced. What their parents say and do, what other people say and do, and what they hear and see on TV constantly influence children's thinking about what is right, wrong, and fair. As they grow up, they adopt many of the behaviors of the people they see and spend time with. It follows that the most influential role models for children are those who spend the most time with them.

The behavior and values your children develop will reflect your beliefs to the degree that you spend time with them and effectively communicate and model those beliefs in your own lifestyle. If you don't take an active role in preparing your children to be thoughtful and make their own decisions by teaching them your values, then they're more likely to be led by what they see at school, out in the neighborhood, or on TV.

Your children are looking to you for direction and guidance. Here's how you can influence their values as they develop:

- **Know your own values**
- **State your values**
- **Make rules that support your values**
- **Help your children think about values**

KNOW YOUR OWN VALUES

We believe that parents need to be more conscious of what their values are, and what affect their actions have on how their children develop their own values. Think about what you really believe in, and what's important to you and your family. Talk your values over with your partner, and develop a shared position on values so the two of you can consistently reinforce those beliefs in your family life. Learn to talk about your values and your feelings, and how your feelings are connected to your values. Don't wait to drift into decisions or until you face a crisis. The things you say and do influence your children—make sure you're having the effect you want.

YOU ARE THE PRIMARY INFLUENCE

As parents you are the primary teachers in your home—by what you say and do. If you want to pass your beliefs and values on to your children, you have to know what your own values are and live by them. You pass on your beliefs best by example rather than by mandate. To serve as an effective example, you must spend time with your child, putting your values into words, talking about how you decided on your values, and behaving based on those values. Use your authority only when you need to take leadership. Then you can say, "This is how it will be." In the long run, your goal is to encourage your child's cooperation with the values you hold dear.

As your children develop, your parental influence will change. Babies are so dependent and needy that parents have absolute control over them. Gradually, parents lose influence until their children enter their teens when their most important influences become their peers and friends. By the time they reach age fifteen or sixteen, your influence will be at a minimum.

Between the ages of eight and twelve years old, there is an important "window of influence"[2] when parents have their best opportunity to influence their kids. At this age, children are learning to be more thoughtful. They're learning to really listen and talk to others and can conceptualize, think abstractly, and make judgments. Children in this eight- to twelve-year-old age bracket are especially open to adopting their parent's values—while they're absorbing everything they see and hear like sponges, their parent's influence is still high.

It is crucial for parents to build communication and trust, and share their values with their children during this stage. Statistics show that the more you influence your children directly about your values on sex, drugs, and alcohol during this period, the later in life they will involve themselves with sex, drugs, and alcohol, and the less intense their involvement will be.

This doesn't mean that you've completely lost your opportunity to influence your child if he or she is over twelve years old. This window of influence can be stretched to the degree that you've developed a good relationship with your children while they're most receptive. This can give your family additional opportunities as your kids reach adolescence.

---

[2] Adapted from Dr. Steven Glenn, "Dealing with the Hostile Child/Adolescent." Audio tape. Hurst, Texas: Humansphere Inc., 1981.

Think about What You Believe In

You might need to clarify your own beliefs and values before you can effectively model them for your children. Ask yourself, "What are my values? What do I believe in? Where did I get my values? What were the biggest influences on me?" Was it church? School? Parents? Grandparents? Friends? Television?

Your values constitute your personal philosophy of life. They are the things, people, ideas, and feelings you care enough about that you will act to gain or keep them. Most people don't give much thought to what their values are. They frequently accept the values of others without really thinking through whether these values really matter to them. Read over the list below. As you read, check the ones that are most important to you.

__ Great car	__ Friends	__ Love
__ Physical fitness	__ Wealth	__ Conversation
__ Respect	__ Good health	__ Nice clothes
__ Education	__ Children	__ Relaxation
__ Beautiful house	__ Clear plans	__ Honesty
__ Flexibility	__ Being attractive	__ Speaking up/ courage
__ Intimacy	__ Good nutrition	__ Nice environment
__ Learning	__ Peace of mind	__ Vitality
__ TV	__ Security	__ Comfortable pace
__ Travel	__ Good books	__ Art/Theater
__ Achieving things	__ Personal growth	__ Close family life
__ Music	__ Religion/Spirituality	__ Sports
__ Humor	__ Pets	__ Hobbies
__ Nature	__ Adventure	__ Challenge
__ Personal planning	__ Good relationship	__ Satisfying work
__ Things working	__ Leisure time	

Your Values about Sex, Drugs, and Alcohol

One of the most important things you can do for your children is to prepare them by passing on your values about sex, drugs, and alcohol. The fact that children are exposed to street drugs as early as elementary school should serve as a warning that harmful influences exist in their world, and that children are at high risk—perhaps at an earlier age than parents think. They need "protection" they can take with them, not just the checks they have when you're there to monitor, control, and guide them, but values they can internalize. When your values become theirs, children have a solid base from which to make conscious decisions about important issues in their lives.

Often, kids learn about sex, drugs, and alcohol from television, movies, and their peers at school, rather than their parents. Peer pressure can influence a child to "do this and be like us"—whether it's wearing certain kinds of clothes, being involved in school activities, drinking, doing drugs, or having sex.

What Is Your Position about Sex? Drugs? Alcohol?

To help you clarify your beliefs or values about sex, drugs, and alcohol, list them in the spaces provided below, and then write down the experience or story that helped you arrive at that belief.

For example:

BELIEF/VALUE

STORY/EXPERIENCE

Cocaine can kill you.

Len Bias, the basketball star, died of a cocaine overdose.

Premarital sex is immoral.

Church teaching

Sex

1. _____   _____

_____

2. _____   _____

_____

Drugs
1. _____   _____

_____

2. _____   _____

_____

Alcohol
1. _____   _____

_____

2. _____   _____

_____

List three values about sex, drugs, and alcohol that you received from your parents.

1. _____

2. _____

3. _____

List one value about sex, drugs, or alcohol that you received from your parents but have rejected.

1. _____

Why did you reject this value?

_____

_____

Life Line

The Life Line form below will help you clarify some of your expectations for your children about relationships, sex, drugs, and alcohol. These represent typical situations where your children's values will be put into action. Next to each of these events, write in the age at which you would like to see your child experience them (one child at a time).

	FIRST CHILD	SECOND CHILD	THIRD CHILD
First date	_____	_____	_____
Drive a car	_____	_____	_____
First kiss	_____	_____	_____
First sexual experience	_____	_____	_____
First drink of alcohol	_____	_____	_____
Smoke	_____	_____	_____
First job	_____	_____	_____
Move away from home	_____	_____	_____
Marry	_____	_____	_____
Become a parent	_____	_____	_____

On a separate page, have each of your children list at what age they think they should have that experience. Use a comparison of the two (or more) lists as the basis for starting a discussion about values. Note: The goal is not to determine which age is right or wrong, but to clarify your expectations or hopes around these issues.

Finally, write down three beliefs or values that you wish to pass on to your children regarding sex, drugs, and alcohol. (For example, what do you think about nudity, dating, and drinking in your home?)

1. _____

2. _____

3. _____

Talk to Your Partner about Your Values

Let's look at some of the issues that force parents to examine and act on their values. Talk these questions and situations over with your partner. Make a decision about what you would do in each situation, and then explain the reasons for your decision. Ask your partner to do the same.

1. At what age would you stop allowing a child to bathe with a parent of the same sex/opposite sex?
2. At what age would you let your child date? What factors about your child would affect your decision?
3. What would you do if you found out that your thirteen-year-old child has smoked marijuana for the first time?
4. What would you do if you found out that your seventeen-year-old has been sexually active for the past year?
5. What would you do if you were at a wedding with your two children, ages ten and twelve, and you saw each of them with a glass of champagne?
6. At what age would you let your child go on a weekend trip with a companion of the opposite sex and his or her parents?

Think about your beliefs and talk them over with one another. What is your belief about drinking alcohol in a family setting? Is it all right if you're having dinner and want to share a little wine with it? Would you allow your children to participate?

Is alcohol allowed in your house? What are your values about alcohol usage? What are your beliefs about the drug use? Talking over your values about sex, drugs, and alcohol will help both of you become aware of where you stand and what issues you may need to negotiate in order to present a unified front to your children.

Tips

- **Take the time to think through what's most important to you in your life.** While everyone has values, most people are vague and uncertain when asked what their values are. It will be easier to communicate your values to your children if you're clear on what they are.

- **Talk your values over with your partner.** Talking about your values helps you to clarify and solidify them. If most individuals aren't sure about their own values, you can imagine how much they know (or don't know) about their partner's!

- **Make sure you and your partner are on the same wavelength about what you want to pass on to your kids.** Parents often have strong feelings about their values—and they don't always agree with one another. It's especially important to work out your differences with your partner before you try to communicate them to your children.

Traps

- **Drifting into decisions.** If you don't have a conscious personal philosophy as a guide for your life, you may lack the direction and certainty you need to guide your children toward developing their own values.

- **Accepting values from others instead of determining your own.** It's up to you to do your own thinking about what matters to you. You cannot be successful and happy relying on others to do your thinking for you.

STATE YOUR VALUES

If you're like most parents, it won't be easy for you to talk to your children about values, especially when it comes to sex, drugs, and alcohol. It's unlikely that you were encouraged to talk about these issues by your parents. Even if you were, you may not have particularly wanted to talk to them about it. It can be awkward for both parents and children. Still, as awkward or uncomfortable as you may be, and as humble as you may feel about knowing what's right, it's both your right and your responsibility to share your values with your kids. Your conversations will be even more difficult if you don't prepare yourself for these issues, only to discover that your children are already having sex or are already using drugs or alcohol. By then, you'll really feel helpless and out of control.

Many parents get ready to talk to their children about these issues before they're really clear on what their values and expectations are. We think it helps to plan ahead—to give yourself the opportunity to think before you speak, and before you get into a situation where you have to state your values unexpectedly. Take the time to think these important topics through so you're clear on what you believe in, and can talk to your children about them. Until you start putting your values into words and stating them out loud, you'll never get used to talking about these often uncomfortable topics.

Talk to Your Children about Sex, Drugs, and Alcohol

List the main points you would make in response to the following questions. Remember to give the information your children have asked for—and the values you associate with it.

1. "Where do babies come from?" asks your five-year-old.

Information: _____

Values: _____

2. "Why do you drink beer?" asks your twelve-year-old.

Information: _____

Values: _____

3. "What's wrong with making yourself feel good with drugs?" asks your thirteen-year-old.

Information: _____

Values: _____

4. "How do you know if you're pregnant?" asks your fourteen-year-old.

Information: _____

Values: _____

Take time to talk over the following questions with your children. Make sure to include discussions of your attitudes about sex, drugs, and alcohol.

1. What do you (child) want to be doing when you're twenty-five years old?
2. What do you think I would want you to be doing at age twenty-five?
3. In what ways do you think you'll be similar to me when you grow up?
4. How do you think you'll be different from me when you grow up?

Respect Your Privacy—and Your Child's

Some parents feel awkward and embarrassed about talking to their kids about sex, drugs, and alcohol because of their own past mistakes. Passing on your values does not mean passing on your history. Do not tell your children about your first sexual experience, or about things you're now ashamed of or don't feel comfortable about like the time you drank too much or used drugs. When your child says, "Didn't you ever do that?" You don't have to say, "Yeah. I did." You should say, "That's not the point here. The point is that your agreement with me is that you won't."

Use Creative Opportunities

Since kids don't usually come to their parents for advice about sex or drugs, you'll need to establish and maintain a dialogue with them that includes what you think about these issues. This way you can be sure to get across your beliefs. Keep in mind that if you don't establish this dialogue, then television, movies, and their peers will be the primary influences on your child's value system.

Parents often wait for the right time to talk with children about sex, drugs, and alcohol. You'll need to find a way to create opportunities to make that connection with them. You can even use awkward situations as opportunities to start this kind of conversation—and send your child the message that they don't have to be afraid to discuss sensitive issues with you.

For example, this conversation:

"George, I was vacuuming your room, and I found this condom. I was wondering if you know what these are for?"

"Oh yeah. All the guys have them. We use them in the shower at the gym. They call them a pink panther, it's a condom."

"These are for having sex so that you don't get someone pregnant or pass on diseases to one another."

"Oh, Mom, I know that stuff. We carry them because then girls will think we're safe, but mostly we just fill them up with water and throw them at each other."

"I like what you said about being safe. It's really good that you have them. I just want you to know that I want you to have a lot of time to grow up before you have children."

"I know Mom. What's for dinner?"

(Kids get anxious talking about sex, and may quickly reach a point where they're not ready to continue talking about it. When they let you know they're uncomfortable, step back and don't keep pursuing it. The important thing is that you can talk openly with one another).

George's mom could've turned this discussion into a lecture, moralized at him, or she could have come on real strong with him. Then, she would have missed the opportunity to hear how he does use condoms, and what he thinks. The best you can do is to make room for him to speak up and for you to speak up. Usually this means taking on less of an authoritarian role and more of the role that we use with other adults to talk together. After all, once they're in their teens, your children are on their way to adulthood.

Get Outside Help If You Need It

We really hope that as parents you'll develop as broad a base as possible for looking at the world with your children. If you don't have the answers you need, get help from the kind of people you'd like to have an influence on your children. If you find it hard to talk about sex or drugs with your children, bring in someone that you trust—your minister, your aunt, your uncle, or a friend—to help you. Read books that give practical advice on the subject. Don't give away the job to the streets.

Here are some examples of the right kind of responses:

"I'm glad you asked about that. I don't know enough to give you a complete answer right now, but I'll check and get back to you."

"Thanks for asking me. This is a hard subject for me to talk about so I need to collect my thoughts and talk to you about it in an hour."

"I want to answer your questions as completely as possible, so I'm going to talk it over with Pastor Brown. Let's talk again in a few days."

Think about who, if anyone (a book, friend, parents, clergy, physician, teacher, counselor, etc.), you could go to for help in each of the following situations:

- Your five-year-old daughter is masturbating in the living room.
- Your son says he has heard that alcohol is more damaging than marijuana.
- Your eight-year-old son complains of pains in his testicles.
- Your child wants to know if a person can get AIDS from kissing.
- Your child wants to know why some people think you should be married before having sex, and others think it's OK without marriage.

Tips

- **Look for opportunities to talk with your child.** Talking with your kids is not always easy. You can just avoid it, but it's better if you give it a try and say something. Think about what you want for your child. Speak up. Listen to what he or she has to say and acknowledge what they tell you.
- **Gear your explanations to the child's age.** Make sure your approach fits their ability to absorb or understand.
- **Respect your own rights to privacy.** You have as much right to privacy as your children have.

- **Recognize your limits in discussing certain issues.** You can anticipate that there will be times when you and your child are unable to talk about some aspect of sex, drugs, or alcohol—either because one of you is uncomfortable discussing the specific issue, or because you feel uninformed on the subject.

Most parents experience this problem at one point or another. You don't need to be an expert on everything, and you can't expect yourself to feel comfortable with every discussion. You're not inadequate, so don't walk away from the situation. Sometimes all you need to do is take a break to give yourself time to think an issue through. If this doesn't work, get help from someone else you respect who might know more about the topic or be able to make some suggestions that would help you discuss it more comfortably.

Traps

- **Giving too much data.** If you're discussing sex, you do not need to give your child a biology lesson. Keep your explanations simple and straightforward—and include your values about it.
- **Not bringing up important topics because you're embarrassed.** Don't count on your child getting accurate information on sex, drugs, and alcohol elsewhere; parents must provide not only the information but the corresponding values as well.
- **Waiting for your children to bring up discussions.** Most children do not ask their parents about sex, drugs, or alcohol, so parents need to look for ways and times to bring up these topics.
- **Telling your kids your war stories from the past.** Sharing intimate details of your own experiences with sex, drugs, or alcohol is inviting them to do the same. Kids learn a lot from the stories that you tell them from your past. You probably also know a lot of stories that reflect the values you do want to share with your kids, and we urge you to share those rather than the ones about your mistakes.

- **Getting sidetracked by separate issues.** By all means, respect your children's privacy, but not at the expense of your important values about their health and safety. In the situation that follows, for example, the daughter is right about her need for privacy, but her possession of drugs is clearly not acceptable.

"I went in and put the laundry in your drawer and found this marijuana. This isn't okay. I'm really angry."

"I'm angry too. You don't have any right to go in my room and look at all my stuff. That's my private stuff. You're treating me like a little baby. Don't you realize I'm fourteen years old now? I need some privacy."

In a situation like this, you want to avoid getting caught up in the privacy issue. Focus on the bigger issue of her having drugs in her room. For example:

> "Your privacy is important, and a bigger issue for
> me right now is our rule that you stay drug free."

MAKE RULES THAT SUPPORT YOUR VALUES

The rules you set for your children should reinforce your values. Rules about privacy, people's property, homework, friends, sex and dating, drugs and alcohol and smoking all reflect your values and expectations for your kids. Just reacting to events as they happen will not give you or your children the structure you need to be clear on what your expectations are.

Think Ahead

As your child grows and develops, you will need to change your rules so that they fit new situations. You may want to think about things like children of the same or opposite sex bathing together. At what age do you need to make some rules about this? What are you comfortable with regarding issues of privacy and nudity? What are your rules about curfew? Spending the night with friends? What are your rules about kids having friends in the house without an adult present? Do you find it consistent with your values to share a glass a wine or beer your children as they get older? If you start preparing your children to use alcohol, do you think this is an invitation for them to drink alcohol?

As children move into junior high and high school, they become more and more like adults. Along with all the physical and social changes they undergo, they also feel a tremendous upsurge of self-centeredness and power. They begin experimenting more, and they should. They've just figured out that they can make a difference and can have an impact on the world, so they're trying it out. They need to have enough autonomy to start getting out on their own, but they still need strong, clear, independent parents who can set limits for them. It's a tricky time for parents, but we think it's better to make rules that you can renegotiate with your children from time to time as they get older and show more responsibility than to wait until there's a crisis. When they start to express interest in sex, drugs, and alcohol, you need to be able to provide a proper model for their behavior.

For example:

> "It's time we faced up to the fact that Jason's voice is changing, he's beginning to shave, and he's definitely interested in girls. When I came home from work today, he and a girl were in his room with the door closed."
>
> "Don't be so hard on him. You're probably just getting all excited about nothing. He's got his video games in there. Maybe they're just playing some games or talking."
>
> "I'm not being hard on him. I just want us to have an agreement about this because I feel very strongly about it. Remember when we were kids. We looked for times to be alone together too, huh?"

"Yeah, but for one thing, we were eighteen, not fifteen. And, I wouldn't want them to be doing what we were doing. Let's make an agreement for now that he can visit with his girlfriends when we're at home, and not at all when we're not here."

"I'm fine with that. That makes a lot of sense."

These issues will continue to come up even when your children are grown. Remember, you set the rules in your home. Your kids can disagree with you and think you're old fashioned, but your values prevail in your home.

For example:

"Jeff and I want to go to the mountains for a weekend, and we were wondering if we could use the cabin?"

"No, I'm not comfortable with that."

"What do you mean? We've been going together for two years. You know we're having sex. It's not like we're going to do anything different."

"I understand that. I appreciate the fact that you have plenty of opportunities to be sexual. However, I'm not ready to publicly support you doing that."

Just Say "No"

One of the most important things you can teach your children is how to say "No." Unfortunately, it's not enough to tell them to "Just say 'no'." In many cases, even adults don't say no when pressured sexually, or to invitations to drink or do drugs. Having clear rules of your own about sex, drugs, and alcohol is the first step in teaching your children to say "No."

Yours might include:

"No drugs whatsoever are allowed."

"No, you cannot have girls/boys in your bedroom."

"No. You are under age, and drinking is illegal."

In addition to the rules you have, your children may need to practice saying "No." You can help them rehearse sample answers to pressure from others:

"No. I like you and I want to be with you but I'm not ready for sex yet."

"No. I'm really not interested in drinking alcohol. I like to have a good time without drinking."

"No. I'm afraid of drugs. I'm against the use of drugs because they're harmful. I know they're not legal, and I don't want to get into trouble."

What If Your Child Doesn't Say "No"?

If your child does experiment with drugs and alcohol, what then? We're sure you'll agree that what comes first is your children's health and safety. They need to know you care enough about them that if they break the rules, your biggest concern is still their health and safety. This is important because if your kid does get high, or into trouble of some kind, you want them to know they can call on you for help.

Here are a few examples of ways you can express your concerns:

"I want you to be alcohol free. I also realize this may be a standard you don't always keep. I don't want to set you up to feel that you cannot tell me things because it's important that we be able to talk things over and be close. Most of all, I value your safety."

"If you drink or do drugs, do not drive. Call us. We don't care what time it is, call and we will come and get you. Call us even if you decide to stay over with a friend to sleep it off. We want to know where you are and that you're safe."

"I want you to be alcohol-free but if you do drink, call me because your safety comes first."

Parents know well the dangers involving sex, drugs, and alcohol and are especially anxious about what to do when their children begin to experiment with them. With so much on the line, it's easy to get into an uproar with your kids when they break your rules. Consider the confrontation that follows between a father and his daughter who comes home late and has been drinking. How would you change what he says and does so it reflects values that are important to you and follows the guidelines we've presented in this book? Plan what you would say if this happened with your child:

> "Lorri, is that you? Fifteen years old and you're coming home at 2 A.M.! We've been worried sick about you. Where have you been? Your mother's upstairs. She cried herself to sleep worried about you. What's the matter with you? Have you been drinking? Let me smell your breath, young lady."
>
> "Nothing is the matter, Dad. Just give me a break. I can't talk right now. I'm tired. I'm going to bed."
>
> "No you're not going to bed. I want to know right now. Now, you listen to me. I've been up all night worrying about you. I've called all around. What happened? Who were you with? Where were you?"
>
> "I just fell asleep at a friend's. It's all right."
>
> "Asleep with whom?"
>
> "We just had a little bit of beer dad. Look, you don't have to worry about me. I can handle it."

More often than not, this girl's parents would start asking her a lot of questions, either because they're anxious or they feel they need to punish her on the spot. This won't accomplish anything, except to escalate the bad feelings between parents and child. In a situation like this one, where you clearly need to take charge, give the child a strong message that you're upset—and buy time to decide what action you'll take. Your child is already tired, embarrassed, and drunk, so this is not the time to start asking a lot of questions.

A better response might be:

"Your curfew was mignight, and our rule is no alcohol. You'll go to bed, and we'll discuss this tomorrow."

Parents need to help each other be prepared for what to say and do next. If your opinions clash, you need to arrive at a compromise. Make a decision about how far you're going to probe. Along with any immediate communication, you need to meet to re-establish your rule and carry through with the consequences for breaking that rule.

When your child is late getting home one night, you're bound to experience worry, frustration, and anger. It's important for parents to talk through the situation together so they don't just react out of anger. Most parents don't especially want to punish their children. They're worried. Parents can also help each other to stay on track when they're really angry. If you're not as upset as your partner, stay on his or her side and do your best to acknowledge their angry feelings, but also hold him/her accountable for proper expression of those feelings. Your partner has reason to be feeling anxious and worried. Acknowledge that. However, keep in mind that parents can scar their children's self-image for years to come with angry outbursts like name-calling.

Your children will challenge you over and over as they go through the process of figuring out where they stand and what they believe in. In response, they need a high degree of self-definition from you. Where do you stand? What do you believe in? You can still have a lot of influence on your kids, even when they reach their teen years, if you can maintain a trusting, communicative relationship.

Tips

- **Make a list of five rules that reflect your values.** Think about curfews, your kids having friends over, sex, drugs, and alcohol.

- **Ask your child to role play with you how to say "No."** Think of a situation your child might be faced with. It can be on a date, responding to an invitation to go to a party where there may be drugs or alcohol, etc.

- **Delay their experimentation with drugs and alcohol as long as possible.** There's a chance that your children will experiment with drugs or alcohol at some point despite all the love and guidance you give them. What you want to be able to do is to delay that experimentation as long as possible by having a trusting relationship, and providing family and social activities and parental supervision. Studies show that the older children are when they first experiment, the less likely they are to get hooked on drugs or alcohol. If you can delay their first drug or alcohol use until after they're eighteen, they have a much better chance of a drug-free or alcohol-free future.

- **Model your values in your own lifestyle.** In any child's life the first models are parents and others that live in the same home. Be a good model for your child.

Traps

- **Expecting kids to "Do as I say, not as I do."** We've all heard this—and it doesn't work. If you think a healthy lifestyle is right for your kids, it's right for you.

- **Angry, destructive outbursts.** Make sure you express your care and concern along with your frustration. Let them know that you care enough about them that if they break a rule, your greatest concern is for their health and safety. If you accidentally respond to your child in a way you wish you hadn't, make sure you take the time to apologize for it later.

"I'm sorry. I don't always do things right. That isn't what I wanted to say. I was just very upset and frightened for your safety."

- **Fighting with your partner over what you should do.** Parents need to be able to talk things over and reach an agreement about how to carry through on consequences. Otherwise, your kids will go do what they want while you sit and fight over what you should do. Or, your teen will get one of you to take his/her side, and you'll have conflicts with both your spouse and your teen.

HELP YOUR CHILD THINK

Today, many parents are out working more than they're home. Despite their work and all the other pressures of family life, parents need to make time to be with their children. As a parent, it's important for you to be around your children to help them think about the experiences they've had at school and what they've seen and heard from other kids and on TV. Giving your children your input gives them another source of information about the world. Try to help them start thinking critically about what they see out in the world. Then, when they encounter new ideas or unfamiliar values from TV or friends, they'll already have a base of knowledge of their own to help them make their own judgments.

Spending time thinking things through with children encourages them to develop their own thinking. You can teach your kids your values by talking to them and reflecting on your shared experiences, explaining how you arrived at a judgment, and putting your judgment into action. Don't wait and expect your children to come and talk to you. They may not do that. You need to get them to join you in conversations about values, and share your opinions with them. That's part of what passing on values is all about. You need to set up opportunities where you can tell them and show them what your beliefs are by your behavior.

Find Out What Your Child Thinks

The best way to keep in touch with what your children think is to create an atmosphere where your children can talk things over with you. They need to know that when they see, hear, or experience something, it's appropriate for them to bring it home—even if it's something you don't like. Sending them the message that, "if you bring certain words or ideas home, I'm going to get really upset," will shut the door on communication. Then they'll go talk these things over with their friends instead.

Let's say your child comes home from school and says, "I saw F U C K written on a fence. What does that mean?" You might say that it's a curse word about a sexual relationship; it's a word people use when they're angry; or it's a swear word that is usually used in an angry or insulting way. The key thing to remember is that one of the ways your kids learn is by your reactions. If you say, "Don't ever let me hear you say that word again," your child will get the message that it's not okay to talk to you about certain things. But if you handle situations like this by giving an explanation that's appropriate for their age, your children will get the message that it's all right to bring things home to you to discuss.

Also, remember that kids learn that certain words have the power to get a big reaction from other people. If you go ballistic when your child uses a curse word, you can count on them using it again—probably at the worst possible moment!

Real Talk

A lot of people think they are passing on their values to their children by giving them lectures and sermons. Telling your children not to talk about touchy subjects or not to do something because it's wrong isn't enough. You pass on your values mainly by the examples you set in your own lifestyle, and occasionally, by what we call "real talk." By sharing their experiences with you, experiences that you talk about and think through together, your children develop their own judgments. In situations where right and wrong are at issue, you can help your children develop their values by giving them clear, specific messages about what you think, how you thought through the situation, and by giving them the opportunity to express their own thoughts without fear of punishment or ridicule.

For example:

"Did you understand what I had to do back there?"

"What did you think about that situation?"

"What do you think should happen now?"

Real talk is very helpful in starting conversations about touchy subjects. Use the skills you learned earlier to speak up and listen. Practice talking with your child about some situation you've gone through together. Talk about how you thought through the situation and what meaning it has for you, and invite your child to do the same while you listen. Make certain that the child can say whatever he/she thinks and feels, and not be criticized, blamed, or ridiculed.

Think about how much more effective the exchange that follows will be than the corresponding lecture on the subject:

"No, I don't want a drink. Thanks. I enjoy being here but I don't need to have a drink to have a good time."

"Dad, what did you do that for? That sounded harsh...."

"I know but this happens all the time. He's always trying to force a drink in my hand like that's gonna make me relax and have a good time. I get more tense the more he offers it. Actually, I have a good time without drinking."

"Yeah, but he was just trying to be nice."

"I know he's trying to be nice in his way. It's just not the way I believe. I don't want to have a drink. I'm sorry it makes you feel awkward but I wanted to tell him how I was feeling. If I have one or two drinks, I get a headache. I don't like that."

"Well, I didn't know why you were saying no. I thought you didn't like him or something."

"No, he's okay. It's just when he keeps pushing at me to have drinks, I start to get upset, and I don't really enjoy being around him when he drinks. My telling him in a loud voice that I didn't want a drink seemed kind of strange, huh?"

"Yeah. But I get it. You're not mad at him. You just don't want him to ask you to have a drink. He didn't listen to you the first time so you were saying, 'Back off, I don't want to have you bugging me like this.'"

"That's it."

Parents often let experiences with their children go by without comment. They're used to reacting, that is, they take action only when events require them to. Real talk helps you respond more creatively. You can consciously take the experiences you share with your child as opportunities to talk about what you were thinking, the problem solving process that you went through, and then ask your child to do the same with you.

Tips

• **Use real talk to get conversations started.** For example, a divorced father might raise a critical issue with his nine-year-old son this way:

"You saw me smile at that woman, and you looked mad. I've been wanting to talk to you about my dating. It's hard for me to talk about. Is it hard for you too?"

• **Talk over TV programs which show values you agree or disagree with.** Television reflects what's going on in the world, and can be an important tool in working with your kids, if used creatively. Children see alcohol consumption presented in a sophisticated, elegant way on TV. "Real talk" gives you an opportunity to discuss your values about using alcohol. Make a list of four TV programs that your child watches that could be the basis of "real talks." What are some of the topics you would like to discuss from each program?

TV Show Topics

1. _____

2. _____

3. _____

4. _____

• **Talk about books and movies.** List four books or movies that you and your child have both read or seen that can be the basis for sharing your values.

Book/Movie Topics

1. _____

2. _____

3. _____

4. _____

- **Listen to your child's point of view, and let him/her know you heard it by repeating it back.** For example:

"You like the idea of having lots of money—like that drug dealer has."

- **If you disagree, point out how you think on the matter and how you arrived at your position without lecturing or preaching.** To continue the example above:

"I'd feel bad about it myself if I made my money through somebody buying something from me that is harmful. I like being proud of my job."

- **Use current situations as the basis for drawing out your child's thinking.** Life presents us with many opportunities to start discussions about values. For example:

"Uncle John was really drunk at the party. I know you heard me say he couldn't drive home. I was wondering what you thought about that."

"What do you think of them having a sexy girl in that beer commercial?"

Traps

- **Avoiding uncomfortable subjects.**
- **Never checking what your child reads or watches on television.**
- **Criticizing your child for having ideas different from your own.**
- **Preaching and lecturing to your child about values and beliefs.**

Every one of these approaches will make it very difficult for you to have the kind of influence you want over your child's values. Your influence is strong, but it has its limits, and friends, the media, and popular culture are clamoring for your child's attention. At the same time, your natural affinity with your children makes you the logical and most effective values educator they can have, if you can avoid these pitfalls.

HOW TO COPE WITH CHANGE IN THE FAMILY

ONE LESSON THAT PARENTS LEARN QUICKLY IS THAT CHANGE IS A CONSTANT AND INEVITABLE PART OF LIFE. Once you've solved a particular family problem, or addressed a specific issue or situation, you can't sit back and relax. You'll need to rethink your rules and relationships to cope as new needs and new problems emerge.

Children change as they grow up, and parents change as they pass through various life stages. Some of life's changes are predictable, and some are not. If you expect changes to occur, you'll be better equipped to deal with the new stresses that come with those changes. Also, if you prepare for the predictable changes, you're more likely to be able to deal with the ones you couldn't predict.

There are three principal dimensions to helping your family learn to deal with change:

- Preparing for predictable changes
- Responding to unpredictable changes
- Learning to cope with change

PREDICTABLE CHANGES: THE FAMILY LIFE CYCLE

Families go through six predictable stages of change as their members develop. Each new stage requires family members to make adjustments in their routines of living. As the family encounters new circumstances, such as a child being born or becoming an adolescent, both parents and children need to develop new skills. Until it changes to meet the new circumstances, the family will be less stable.

In most cases, it's easy to identify which stage your family is in. We'll start by looking at the step that "sets the stage" for the others—the period of change that starts as an older child becomes an adult, and prepares to start a family of his/her own.

Young Adults

Leaving home is not a one-step process. It takes many steps, each of which either moves you back toward your childhood or forward into your adult life. Even though you're bound to lapse occasionally, your goal should be to continue making progress in shifting the responsibility for your life from your parents to you. Sometimes parents help foster your independence, and sometimes they don't. Either way, your job is to grow up.

Here's an example of one young adult going through this transition:

Jory had been working as a mechanic until he got frustrated with the boss and quit. His dad says he's immature and hot-headed. Jory thinks he was right to leave that job, but he isn't sure what he wants to do next. He has enough money saved to tide him over for two months. His dad is dead set on Jory going to electronics school next semester. Jory has played along with his dad's idea, but really has no intention of following it. Today, he went over and told his dad that he needs his encouragement, but not his advice. It was hard for Jory to talk so firmly to his dad, but he felt much better after he did.

Tips

- **Work out an adult-to-adult relationship with your parents.** The more you commit yourself to your own path, the easier it is to establish an adult-to-adult relationship with your parents. When you act like a mature person, you are more likely to be treated like one, even by the people who changed your diapers.
- **Develop friendships.** Adults need friends. The companionship and resources friends offer one another helps them hold onto their adult status. Without friends, you tend to feel lonely and like an unwanted little kid.

For example:

Jaime thought about his father every day but hadn't seen him since leaving home at seventeen. Mostly, he remembered how his father left his mother when Jaime was ten years old, and how infrequently he came to visit. He finally decided to look up his father. They had a fight, and Jaime left furious.

Later, he talked about it with an old high school friend. His friend invited him to go to his gym and work out with him. It didn't make Jaime's problem disappear, but it helped to talk with someone who listened.

- **Establish yourself at work.** Everyone needs to have purpose in their life and be productive. Discover what kind of work has meaning for you and find a way to get involved in it. Your overall plan must include providing for your food and shelter. You may want to join with others and divide up responsibilities equitably—or live independently.

For example:

> Judy and three of her friends moved in together last year. They share expenses. Judy does all the cooking and shopping in exchange for a smaller portion of the rent. She keeps her expenses low so she can devote maximum time to her photography, which she hopes to turn into a profit-making business.

- **Use time alone to work on your personal growth.** Single adults are alone more than couples, families, or single parents. They may not, however, be more lonely. Living alone gives you the advantage of being able to spend time working on yourself. It is easier to see and claim the results of your own actions if you're living on your own.

For example:

> Tricia thought of herself as being inept with money until she lived alone for a year. Without her father to do her budgeting for her, she was forced to take it on herself. She was surprised to find that she was good at it.

Traps
- **Depending on your parents to help you feel good about yourself.** Part of growing up is discovering how to make yourself happy—how to find, on your own, the work and relationships that you feel good about.

- **Drifting from one job or one relationship to the next, never figuring out what you really want out of life.** Your values in life don't just come to you. It takes work, planning, and introspection to create the life you want instead of the one that just happens to you.

- **Blaming your parents for all your problems.** Everyone has some unresolved issues left over from growing up. But you can only hold your parents responsible for so long. If you're in your thirties and still talking about how your parents messed you up, it's time to start working out your problems so you can move on.

Couples

While the couple's stage can be a wonderful time, it's also a time of dramatic change. In the chapter on couples, we talked about some of the challenges you face as you build your life with another person. Whether you're changing from living with your parents, living as a single adult, or remarrying, you'll have to make adjustments to include your new partner in your life. Living cooperatively requires that you and your partner commit to facing life together as a team, achieve a balance between pursuing your individual interests and being involved with each other, and negotiate a balance of power where you can count on one another for support and you both feel like you're getting a good deal.

The principles you learned in the chapter on couples hold true anytime you go through the changes and challenges couples face. Whether you're having a baby, moving, going back to school, or starting a new career, you'll experience real stresses and pressures in your relationship that will require changes. You may not have the same amount of time together. Your financial situation may change. In each case, you'll need to commit or recommit yourself to living cooperatively, to keeping some "glue" in your life as a couple while you're also doing things that are important to you as an individual.

Let's suppose that your partner is putting a lot of energy into starting a new career. Both of you need to recommit to living cooperatively. Otherwise, you may end up with the sole responsibility for the connection in your relationship. That won't work—because you'll resent it.

It's vitally important that both you and your partner feel able to talk about what you're feeling. You may have trouble finding the "right" time to talk, and censor what you have to say. Withholding your feelings inevitably creates distance in a relationship. As difficult as it may be, you need to be able to say, "I know you have a career to pursue and that it's very important to you and to us. At the same time, I'd like some time with you. I miss you, and I need for us to have some time together."

People are often concerned that if they give in to this kind of request for connection, they might have to give up too much. Many couples evade or fight about this issue, but you need to acknowledge and recommit yourselves—as a couple—to the connection and closeness that keeps a couple together. Hopefully, your partner's response will be along these lines: "I'm sure glad to hear you say that. I get caught up in my work but I just want you to remember that you're the most important thing in my life. I don't have a lot of time now, and I appreciate how you're hanging in there with me and understanding that. I'm glad you tell me when you need more time because the last thing I want is for you to feel like you're out there by yourself—and resenting it."

When you get the closeness you want, make sure you appreciate and honor it. Getting your way isn't as important as getting the closeness you need. It doesn't take much time to say, "Thank you for being willing to stay connected to me."

Tips

- **Commit yourself to living cooperatively.** Let your partner know that you're willing to make the changes and compromises necessary to living as a couple.

- **Be more your spouse's partner and less your parents' child.** Often your closest connection—up until the time that you choose your first partner—is with your parents. Whether or not you're living with them, you're used to their being there to support you in times of distress and share your joys in happier times. As part of a couple, though, you need to change your emotional connection to focus on your partner.

- **Help your family and friends include your partner.** This is one of the spots where people often get stuck. It isn't always easy for your friends or your family to include a new person. Remember, they don't know your partner as well as you do. Maybe they just don't know how to include someone new. It is your responsibility to take the lead and help your family and friends find ways to be with you and your new partner in ways that everyone finds satisfying.

Here's an example of how one couple handled this:

"Mom, Kathy wants to come over with me from time to time to visit you, but we also want you to come to our house. We want to start some of our own traditions at our house and do things as a family, and we'd like to include you."

Traps

- **Taking your relationship for granted once you're married.** When you were dating, you and your partner spent a lot of time focusing on each other. Once you're married, you must continue to create good times together to keep the relationship alive.

- **Getting caught in the middle between your partner and your family.** Disconnecting from your family to make room for your connection with your spouse can be a difficult adjustment.

As they try to preserve both connections, many couples feel pulled in too many directions. If you spend too much time on your relationship with your relatives—your relationship with your partner may suffer.

• **Doing too much of your own thing and not enough with your partner.** This issue affects most relationships to some degree—you need to balance your need to be separate with your responsibility for spending time, energy and effort on your relationship with your partner.

Along Comes Baby

Once you are expecting a child, massive changes are set in motion. Your mind begins to spin out stories of what might lie ahead.

"We will need a bigger house and more income."

"He will be such a good Dad."

Your feelings run from love to fear to excitement and anticipation.

"She's so wrapped up in the baby. Will she still care about me?"

Further, you find that having a baby is a very social event that frequently results in complicated and unexpected surprises.

"I told Dad that we'll probably name the baby after him. I guess I should've waited until you and I talked more, but I knew he would be so pleased. You're mad aren't you?

Every couple is bowled over by the flood of changes that comes with the birth of the little angel. The physical changes alone are daunting. Sleep deprivation and postpartum blues abound. New parents typically go from their greatest emotional highs to astounding lows over and over again in the first year of their child's life. Adding to the family of two, the needs of this third, very loud person, requires accelerated degrees of self discipline, delayed gratification, personal commitment, and couple and extended family coordination.

Amidst the whirlwind of changes during this time, there are three essential elements that loving families build into the foundation of their lives with children. First, be parents together. Parenting is too hard to do alone, too important to walk away from, and too complicated to fight over. Second, speak up for what you want for your child to their grandparents. Help establish that grandparents (and aunts and uncles) are treasured, neither to be left out nor invited to take over. Third, protect your life as a couple. Carve out time to be together. Do things that reassure your partner of your love.

Tips

- **Be parents together.** When you have a baby, both you and your partner need to become parents. This may sound easy but it isn't. Our normal uncertainty about parenting frequently shows up by our being either over-involved or not involved enough. For example, if mom handles her insecurity by over-connecting with her infant and Dad handles his insecurity by standing back, they can quickly get out of sync. Mom feeling too alone and Dad feeling shut out is fertile ground for blaming. New parents need to talk daily to get a reading of how they are doing as a parenting team and make little adjustments that encourage each other to work together.

"I don't know the first thing about babies," says Kirk defensively as his wife asks him to hold their two-week-old son, Zeke. "Every time I pick him up, he starts crying. I'm just not good at this."

"I know what you mean. I don't like it when he cries when I pick him up either. I get worried that maybe I'm doing something wrong. But I'm beginning to get used to his ways. Let's learn together."

"Yeah, I want this kid to know his dad. When you're finished nursing, let me know. I'll walk with him for awhile before I leave for work."

• **Speak up to grandparents.** As you go through the changes of becoming a parent, often your parents and brothers and sisters are making plans for their new role as grandparents or aunts or uncles. It is a good idea for you to talk with them and reassure them of their importance in your life and that of your child. Make your wishes about childrearing known, listen to what they want, and cooperate to work out differences. These can be informal talks. Don't wait until there is a problem to get the habit in place. Just keep your focus on reassuring them and establishing yourselves as leaders in your own family. If you just "let things happen," you are liable to find yourself resenting them for how they do things without ever having told them what you want. Exercising your own rights and responsibilities as adults and parents while managing your relationships with your extended family is an important and ongoing job.

"Dad, twice this week, you've told me how hard it is on mom to keep Alicia. I need to talk to you about that. Mom tells me she's happy to have Alicia, but I'm not sure you are."

"Well, what if something happened? I love to have her over when she's feeling well. But when she's sick, I think your mom gets too nervous. Since I can't drive anymore, I worry about how we could get her to the doctor if something happened."

"I see. You want to be sure there's a way to get help if needed. I'm glad you told me what's on your mind. I want you both to be happy with the arrangements we make so you'll look forward to having time with Alicia and not be worried about it. Let's sit down and think this through together."

• **Protect your life as a couple.** Often when couples have a new baby, it is so consuming there seems to be very little time left for each other. You may get up at three, four, and five o'clock in the morning, plus spend a lot of time during the day to take care of the baby's needs. It's very important during this time in your life as a family to keep some special time for the two of you as a couple. Stay connected to one another as well as connected to your children.

"Do you need to work late again tonight?"

"Yes, at least until seven. I know it's been rough lately. I miss dinner with the kids. Let's plan a family day on Saturday."

"Well, I've been working overtime too. I want some time for all of us, but I also want some time for just you and me."

"The last time we went out to dinner alone, we just talked about Morgan's colic and worried about the babysitter."

"Yes, it's hard to switch gears and focus on us. It's getting a little easier now that he's six months old and over the colic. Let's try again to get some alone time. I miss you."

"It really feels good to hear you say you miss me. I miss you too. I think even when we're here at home, I need to tell you how important you are to me."

Traps

• **Trying to protect your child from your partner.** A new mother learns a lot about what her baby needs by trial and error in those first few months. It's normal for her to feel responsible and protective. But if she's critical too often as her partner is learning how to parent in his way, she'll discourage his efforts to connect with their child.

For example: Comment on what your partner does right and save your judgments for extreme cases. This will encourage him to stay involved.

"Look how much he enjoys your bouncing him! It's fun seeing you two laugh together."

Instead of:

"Be careful. You can't bounce him around like that after he's eaten. He's not a football. Here let me have him."

• **Leaving all the parenting to your partner.** Some fathers avoid parenting, leaving their mate to take up the slack. This almost always creates resentment.

For example:

"Can't you get the kids to be quiet? You know I'm trying to watch the game."

"Maybe if you spent a little time with them, they wouldn't have to try so hard to get your attention."

As Children Grow

Children's needs keep changing as they get older, and each new stage of their development puts new demands on their parents. A toddler's needs are different from those of a newborn, and the child going off to school has still different needs. Little children need adults to watch over them closely. As they get older, they still need their parents to watch over them, but more from a distance.

One of the most challenging times for both parents and children is often adolescence. It's not unusual for the teenager to challenge the parent who has taken on more responsibility for the child's growing years. It's common for one parent—often the mother—and the teen to be locked in battle over who's in charge, while the father stands by amazed and often critical of his wife. To resolve this problem, the mother must step back more from the everyday duties of raising her child, and the father must involve himself more in the process.

Here's an example of how one family handled this transition:

Elaine used to call her fourteen-year-old son, Brian, six or eight times in the morning to get him up for school. By the fourth time she would be yelling. By the sixth time, they'd both be yelling. He would miss his bus, and she would then drive him to school chastising him all the way while he got more and more sullen. In the evening, she would see him listening to music when he was supposed to be doing his homework, and the fracas would start all over again. It hurt Elaine to lose the sweet, friendly Brian she used to know. She felt lonely, and misunderstood by him. She went to her husband, Victor, and asked him to work with her on the problem.

Victor wasn't very sympathetic to Elaine's complaints about Brian. For the past year, he had watched her crowd their son. The few times he did offer his opinions, Elaine felt criticized and lashed back at him with accusations about his working too much. But, now, Victor was worried too. He wanted peace in their home, and wanted Brian to succeed in school. This time he thanked Elaine for coming to him, and suggested they go together and talk with the school counselor. Until that time, they decided Victor would handle any contact with Brian about his homework.

Tips

• **Stick together.** Parents need to stick together more than ever when they have an adolescent. This can be the most tumultuous time in a family's life. When the kids are little, you can control them fairly easily but teenagers can really press the issue of "who's in charge." Teenagers can become intent on proving that they run their own lives. They've reached the age where they feel grown-up in many ways. Often, they think their parents are out of touch, and that they know more about how things should be than their parents do.

• **Show teens how to work cooperatively by asking them to contribute their ideas along with yours.**

For example:

"Your taste in movies is different from ours! Maybe we can think of something different to do together. Let's each think of two things that we think would be fun, and then compare notes."

• **Allow the adolescent room to come and go.** Teenagers need to be able to belong in the family and yet become more independent. This means that parents will need to make room for them to step out and then step back into the family—bringing with them hair styles, music, attitudes, and friends of their choice. Parents need to be flexible enough to let their children go out on their own, and return with some of their world, to be shared, or at least tolerated, without criticism.

For example:

Terri's friend, Tasha, has dyed her hair green. Terri's dad is horrified.

"If you still want a place to sleep, you'd better get that weirdo out of our house, and keep your hair the way you were born with it."

"It's my hair. I'll do what I want, Dad. Tasha's my best friend."

Later that night, Terri's dad thought things over. He realized that Terri is doing much of what he hoped she would do. She's getting good grades in school and helping out at home. She's also doing a few things he wishes she wouldn't, like openly opposing his views more, wearing a lot of makeup, and maybe dying her hair! He decided not to say anything else about the hair issue and to let Terri know more often what he appreciates about her.

- **Gradually share more decision-making.** It's important to gradually begin to share some of the decision-making processes with teenagers. As they demonstrate more responsibility, give them more of a voice when it comes to decisions about them. They are very close to becoming adults, and being able to share some of the responsibility for decisions is an essential part of their growing experience.
- **Start to focus more on yourself, your marriage, and your aging parents.** Parents need to prepare for the fact that their children are going to be leaving home by gradually shifting their focus

from their children's lives to their own interests and their relationship as a couple. Often, they've spent so much time of their time together focusing on raising kids, that they've lost touch with their individual interests and drifted apart as a couple.

Traps

- **Getting defensive when your teens assert themselves.** A common step in teens defining themselves is to assert that who they are is who you aren't. Don't get defensive—just agree that you're different. You'll need to use your listening skills over and over again with teens. It reassures them that you hear their independent voice and lays the groundwork for operating in a more adult-to-adult and less parent-to-child manner.

- **Over-involvement in your teen's life.** As their children become more autonomous and need less hands-on care, parents may feel like they're being laid off from a job they held for many years. Even when this change is welcome, parents may feel a sense of loss and disorientation as they switch gears from being parents of children to parents of adults. The most difficult aspect of the change is emotional. Even if you're intellectually ready for your children to grow up, you may try to hold on emotionally. It's difficult to give up the satisfaction that comes from having someone who needs you, talks with you, and looks up to you.

Adults with Adult Children

One of the bittersweet experiences of being parents is that if you've done a good job, your kids will be prepared to leave you when they reach adulthood. You might feel as if you had helped them train for adulthood, and now they've graduated. You carried them in your arms as babies, shared their accomplishments, joys, and troubles throughout their childhood. Now it's time to let go of the teacher/student roles you played to carve out new ones. You saw earlier that having a new baby causes the family to reorganize. There's a similar need for instant change when a family member leaves.

Parents can use how they act with their adult friends as a guide to shifting to an adult-to-adult relationship with their adult children. While you have too much symbolic importance to your children to ever be their friend in exactly the same way, you can still use these friendships as a guide. This will help you to keep seeing your adult child as an adult and treating him or her like one, even when it's tempting to fall back into a parental role.

Tips

- **Expect adult children to become more involved outside of the family than in it.** If you have been especially close to your child, expect to feel left out. Both parents and kids need to develop adult-to-adult ways to accomplish the two things that are the hallmarks of healthy family relationships—to both be independent and still be connected to one another.

- **Support your adult child's relationship with a partner.** No matter how old your children, they always want (either secretly or openly) your approval. Make room for the new families they create, the partner they choose, their in-laws, and grandchildren. Expect them to want to set up new rituals to establish themselves as a family. When adult children develop a new source of emotional sustenance, they need you less. As they take a mate for life, do your best to heal old injuries and offer your blessings. If you have recently lost your partner through death or divorce, you may find it harder to graciously make room for a new special person in your child's life. It will get easier as you re-establish your own life.

- **Spend time together because you choose to, not by demand.** Your parent/child relationship has been replaced, in most aspects, by an adult-to-adult relationship more like that of your other friendships.

- **Show an interest in their life and expect them to take an interest in yours.** Make sure there is give and take. You speak and listen, and they speak and listen.

- **Give advice only when asked for it.** Showing respect for and acceptance of their control over their independent life will minimize friction over issues of autonomy—and make it possible for them to come to you for help when they do need it.

Traps

- **Letting your adult children off the hook from their agreements.** If your daughter agrees to water your plants while you're away on vacation, and she doesn't do it, and never mentions it, she's inviting you to treat her like an irresponsible child. Be careful not to let her off the hook with, "She forgets easily," or "I didn't really expect her to come all the way over here just to do that," or "Ever since she's been little, she's hated to do chores." It's better to say, "You had an agreement with me to water the plants. I get angry when you don't keep our agreements. I want to be able to count on you."

- **Filling your time with their life.** If your adult children repeatedly invite you to step in and take care of their problems, resist the temptation. This will only delay their independence—and yours. Most young adults will mature if their parents refuse to play along with their immature behavior, and show their appreciation in areas where their children are mature.

- **Prying.** When your children are beginning to establish their adult life, be available if they need a friend to talk to, but focus more on your interests and general topics. Be cautious about asking too much about them. Wait for them to volunteer information, especially on "hot" topics. Other people can get by with asking about what they did over the weekend, if they have a girlfriend, if they have a job yet. But if you ask those same questions, it may sound like you're questioning their ability to run their own life. Even if you do have questions, it won't help for you to ask them. They are not self-possessed enough to be able to reassure you about your concerns.

The Golden Years

The stages of family life conclude with the family entering later life. As you age, and your children take on their adult lives, you reverse roles with them. They need less caretaking, and you need more. It can be humbling to get in touch with how vulnerable you are to their good will, how much you rely on them to be sensitive to your needs. You no longer have the advantage you had when they were little and would "do it because I told you to." To be a healthy family with adult children, all members must rely more and more on mutual caring and cooperation, rather than on coercion and obligation.

Tips

• **Maintain your own interests and develop ones as a couple that acknowledge changing physical abilities.** As you grow older, it is still important to stay active and involved. You may need to consider modifying or adapting your activities so that you can maintain as much independence as possible.

• **Accept and support a more central role of adult children.** You may need physical, emotional, and financial support—and you may need to accept guidance and decision-making support from your adult children. While this role reversal may be difficult to adjust to, it also provides new opportunities for working cooperatively with your family members.

• **Deal with the nearness of your own death and that of friends and family members.** No one likes to think about their own death, but part of your responsibility as an aging adult is to do what you can to make sure your death isn't an oppressive financial or emotional burden on your family or friends.

Traps

- **Overdoing for elderly parents.** Adult children, often in the middle of raising their own family, sometimes try to take on too much responsibility for the care of their aging parents. It's necessary for them to strike a balance between providing care and support and leaving your parents with as much independence and self-sufficiency as possible.

- **Not respecting the rights and the wisdom of elderly parents.** Older family members have accumulated a lifetime of experience—and have spent most of their lives in the role of independent, responsible adults. Be sensitive that your attempts to help might be misinterpreted as intrusive or inconsiderate.

- **Avoiding each other because of disagreements on how things ought to be done.** This is a time when you can give something back to parents who have always been there for you. This is not the time to get stubborn or inflexible with each other.

- **Refusing to allow adult children to give you input on what to do.** It's often difficult for parents to accept advice from their adult children, as this example shows:

"I've managed my own affairs all my life. I'm not stopping now. I plan to die with my boots on! Why should you be coming over here, telling me what to do?"

SPECIAL FAMILY CHANGES

While change is a normal part of life, it isn't always predictable. In fact, it can sometimes be upsetting and painful. It's particularly difficult when the change is brought on by circumstances beyond your control. The reality is that when people or situations around you change, you need to choose how you're going to change as well.

While some families go through the entire cycle of predictable stages we've described, many do not. Today, there are large numbers of families who go through the exceptional changes of divorce, single parenting, and the blending of families. These families need to make special adjustments or changes to stay healthy through these special family stages.

Divorce with Co-parenting

Sometimes partners split up. As hard as they may have tried, some parents just can't make their relationship as a couple work. This is a difficult time for both parents and their children. The challenge in this stage is for the parents to be able to separate their parenting relationship from their couple's relationship so the children can have ongoing contact with both parents.

Tips

- **Conclude your spousal agreements with as much dignity and benevolence as you can.** The less anger or resentment you take away from the process of dissolving the relationship, the more likely you are to be able to make a co-parenting arrangement work with your ex-spouse.

- **Ensure that children keep ties to both of you.** While it can be very difficult for couples to get beyond the anxiety, hurt, and anger of losing their relationship, it is generally best for children to have ongoing contact with both parents.

- **Each parent takes charge in their own household.** It helps if the co-parents can agree on certain rules so there is some consistency for the kids as they move back and forth between the two households. We recognize that the couple might not be divorced had they been able to work through problems and negotiate rules they could both agree on. Given that reality, we suggest that each parent agree that the other has the right to make the rules in his or her own household.

Traps

- **Dragging out hostilities.** The children who fare the worst after a divorce are those whose parents keep fighting each other.

- **Continuing your battles through your children.** Trying to get back at your ex by making negative comments to your children will only hurt your children, make them angry, or make them feel like they have to choose sides. Don't ask your children to make a choice that can deprive them of a parent.

- **Trying to control how your ex-spouse parents the kids.** Typically, even married parents find it difficult to get each other to do things their way. If you're divorced, forget about trying to have that kind of influence. Step in only if your child's safety is at stake.

Single Parent with No Co-parent

Single parents have an extra burden—trying to fulfill all the responsibilities of raising their children on their own. Two people working together have more power than a child, and each parent and each child literally have an additional person they can go to for support. Single parents and their children in many cases have no where else to go.

Tips

- **Stay in charge.** This can be even more difficult when it's just you and the kids. You have to consistently give the kids a clear message of what the rules are and follow through on enforcing them.

- **Know what you want.** Know the direction you want your family to go. That's where your power is, and how you can best lead your family. It's all right to set limits on your kids. It's also all right that they seem to resist and resent you. You'll undoubtedly make some decisions your kids won't like, but it's essential that you maintain a level of authority that enables you to enforce your rules.

- **Rely heavily on friends and relatives as consultants.** While it's important to have a close relationship with your kids, they cannot take the place of adult companionship and support. Trying to be best friends with your children is a mistake. Make sure you have at least one close adult friend who is sensible and reliable that you can go to when you're in doubt or just need someone to talk to. You may be doing a lot of things right, but you also need someone else to tell you that. The kids don't have the life experience to give you that kind of reassurance. You need an outsider who knows enough about your life to reassure you in a very specific way, to say "you're doing OK" or "that sounds perfectly reasonable to me."

Traps

- **Undercutting your parental authority.** Many single parents find it difficult to balance their roles of guiding and encouraging children. Their tendency is to try so hard to have a close relationship with their kids—to make it up to them for not having another parent—that they lose their ability to set limits and stay in charge.

- **Feeling helpless about staying in charge of your kids as they get bigger.** A lot of parents are concerned that their children are getting bigger than they are. It's true that adolescents can escalate an argument dramatically when you say "no," and it can be frightening to be on the other side of that escalation. But size has nothing to do with staying in charge. We've seen tiny mothers take care of hulking sons and imposing fathers absolutely taken over by small children. If you have been very clear in your messages to your children all along the way, they'll continue to do what you say as they grow older.

- **Using adult household members as co-parents rather than advisors or helpers.** Remember, your friends or family can be your consultants, but it's still up to you to make decisions that are right for you.

- **Trying to do everything on your own.** When you're feeling trapped and alone, be willing to ask for help.

Blended Families

Blended families (stepfamilies) face a complex variety of issues. The children of both spouses may be moving back and forth between their moms and dads, and there may be biological sisters and brothers living together with stepsisters and stepbrothers. The challenges for the couple are to learn to live with one another, co-parent one another's children, and work out arrangements so that the children can maintain their contacts with their natural parents and grandparents. The children also need to develop a relationship with the new stepparent and with their new stepbrothers and stepsisters.

A typical pattern in stepfamilies is that the biological parent thinks the stepparent is too tough on the kids and tries to protect them. At the same time, the stepparent thinks the natural parent is being "too nice" and doesn't hold the line on the kids. This way the stepparent becomes the "heavy" and the biological parent becomes a "pushover." You have to learn to tolerate each other's styles of handling the kids, be willing to back each other up, think through each situation together, allow yourself to stumble and get back up, and preserve some kind of compassion for each other in the process. Kids in blended families typically test the resiliency of the couple's relationship for about two years.

Tips

- **Make a commitment to your new relationship.** Some people try to get involved or get their romantic partner involved in parenting before they even know they're going to stay together. Bringing casual partners into parenting relationships with your children is a mistake. Your children haven't even had the chance to get to know them, much less care about them or respect their authority.

- **If possible, divorced parents should maintain co-parenting agreements.** Make sure children continue to have access to both parents, to the stepparent and to grandparents.

- **Adults should take charge of all children in the household cooperatively.** One of your first challenges as a parent in a blended family is to work out agreements about the rules and expectations of the children. It helps if you can get past ideas like "my kids" and "your kids," and move on to "our rules" for the children in "our home." Decide what your rules are, and be clear that you're going to enforce them together.

- **Allow two years minimum for a new family to consolidate.** These are complicated situations, and patience is a parent's greatest advantage in helping your new family make the transition.

Traps

- **Jumping into the parent role too quickly.** Start out with the biological parent doing most of the enforcement, always backed up by the stepparent. Gradually, work up to both people being in charge.

- **Trying to replace the child's mother or father.** You aren't the new mother or father of these children. Make it clear to them that you are a responsible co-parent, that you could never replace their mother or father, and you want them to maintain a close relationship with their biological parent.

- **Undercutting your partner as a stepparent.** Be clear that the two of you are a team, and you're going to support one another in making and enforcing rules. Otherwise, when the stepparent tries to enforce a rule, the kid(s) will know right where to go to undercut him or her.

- **Tiptoeing around the kids.** Kids sometimes think they can take advantage of a stepparent, because they know he or she wants to be a good parent and doesn't want any conflict with them.
- **Not spending time together away from the kids.** Issues with your kids can become overwhelming. It's very important to balance that by spending time together—just the two of you—away from the kids.

LEARNING TO COPE WITH CHANGE

Family health depends upon the ability to adapt to change as needed. It's helpful to think of learning to deal with change as adding skills and experiences to your family—much like adding rooms onto a house. You may start out with a small house, but as your family grows and you have three, four, or five kids, you have to build onto your house to make it fit your changing needs. Similarly, you may already have some "change" skills, but when change occurs these may suddenly not work as well anymore. So you'll need to build or add on some additional skills to meet your family's growing needs. You'll learn new ways of looking at things, and how to approach problems in a slightly different way. This kind of change occurs gradually on an as needed basis.

Change is part of the natural rhythm of life. But even though change is completely normal, it can still be disruptive. Family stress increases when change is needed, but has not yet occurred. When you or others in your family find yourself becoming more irritable, arguing, thinking negatively, sleeping too much or too little, wanting to eat a lot or not wanting to eat anything, these are all symptoms that something's going on that requires change.

Stress increases as problems linger. Arguing is an indicator that you're stuck. This may mean that you need to expand your repertoire of problem-solving skills.

For example, look at the following conflict:

"You know we're going to need more money when we have the baby. What about your job? How long do you think you can keep working while you're pregnant?"

"I talked to my friend Marsha. She's had three kids now. She said not to worry in this first trimester. It's really basic."

"What did she say about your staying at work because we have to worry about this money thing. I mean, I'm glad you're already concerned about the baby and taking care of yourself and all that."

"Is this the way you're going to be all the time when we have kids? Strictly business? Why don't you just think about the baby instead of about money?"

"I wish you'd think about my worries. I am thinking about the baby. I'm thinking about us."

"That's not what it sounds like to me. Oh, come off it. I'm really excited about having a baby, and I'd like you to get excited with me. You act like the most important thing is how long I'm gonna keep working. What do you want me to do? Keep working forever and just let this kid grow up on its own?"

"No, I think it's good that you work so we have enough money to do things like having a baby."

"Now don't give me that. We talked about it ahead of time."

"Sure we did, but look at the way we are right now. We're starting to hassle each other. We've been doing this more in the past couple of weeks."

"I'm not hassling. You're the one that's hassling."

These two haven't been parents before, and there are some things they haven't worked out. He's worried about security and providing for the family, and she's more focused on her body and taking care of the baby. She resents him a little bit and decides that he's not very understanding but thinks, "What can you expect? Men don't understand about children. They don't have them in their bodies." And he'll figure, "She really doesn't love me. What she wants is security, and so it's my job as a man to provide that for her." There's a whole gamut of reasons they can now use to justify moving slightly apart from one another. And if they do, they won't be able to preserve the level of intimacy they want.

This kind of tension is normal, but they're stuck nonetheless. Now, they have a choice to make. They can read the signals and say, "Something is wrong here. We are getting stuck." They can recognize that they're reaching a crisis and work toward a resolution, or move away from the difficulty without resolving it, or it can escalate into a bigger crisis. This happens sometimes very openly and dramatically and sometimes rather subtly.

In any case, the tension they're feeling is an indication that it's time for a change to occur in their relationship.

Even though it's awfully hard to accept some changes, change is most harmful when you cannot move through the resistance and find new ways of doing things. For example, consider a twenty-four-year-old who demands that his parents "help him out" when he can't afford the apartment he would like. If his parents give in to his demands, they may actually be helping him establish a continuing pattern of dependence on them. Another example would be a sixty-year-old woman who pouts and cries when her daughter's family doesn't include her on their vacation. If her daughter gives in to her to "make grandma happy," she is not successfully establishing an adult-to-adult relationship with her mother. In each of these examples, an important stage of family development is being impeded by their resistance to change.

Everyone faces some level of stress in their life. Some levels are easy to manage, while others may require outside help.

Stress Levels

The following test measures life events in terms of their impact in "Life Change Units."[3]

1.	Death of a spouse	100
2.	Divorce	73
3.	Marital separation	65
4.	Jail term	63
5.	Death of a close family member	63
6.	Personal injury or illness	53
7.	Marriage	50
8.	Fired at work	47
9.	Marital reconciliation	45
10.	Retirement	45
11.	Change in health of family member	44
12.	Pregnancy	40
13.	Sexual difficulties	39
14.	Gain of a new family member	39
15.	Business readjustment	39
16.	Change in financial state	38
17.	Death of a close friend	37
18.	Change to different line of work	36
19.	Change in number of arguments with spouse	35
20.	Foreclosure of mortgage or loan	30
21.	Change in responsibilities at work	29
22.	Son or daughter leaving home	29
23.	Trouble with in-laws	29
24.	Outstanding personal achievement	28

---

[3] Adapted from Holmes, T.H. and Rabe, R.H. "The Social Readjustment Rating Scale," *Journal of Psychosomatic Research* 11 pp. 213-218. Pergamon Press, 1967.

25.	Spouse begins or stops work	26
26.	Begin or end school	26
27.	Change in living conditions	25
28.	Revision of personal habits	24
29.	Trouble with boss	23
30.	Change in work hours or conditions	20
31.	Change in residence	20
32.	Change in schools	20
33.	Change in recreation	19
34.	Change in church activities	19
35.	Change in social activities	18
36.	Change in sleeping habits	16
37.	Change in number of family get-togethers	15
38.	Change in eating habits	13
39.	Vacation	13
40.	Christmas	12
41.	Minor violations of the law	11

Add up the number of life change units you're currently experiencing. If you scored 150-199, you're going through a mild life crisis; 200-299, a moderate life crisis; or 300+, a major life crisis.

What's most important is that there be a balance between the amount of stress you're experiencing and the resources you have to draw upon to help. The bottom line is that when you're going through difficult life changes and feel out of control or need some help, you have to look for it.

Tips

• **Expect change.** As you've already seen, you might as well expect change. Just as you're beginning to get your life established in one way, some other aspect of it will change. Many of those changes are predictable results of the growth and development of your family such as a child being born, beginning school, reaching adolescence, or leaving home. Anticipating change can help you minimize many of its painful and damaging effects.

- **Stress is a signal change is needed.** Pay attention, because the symptoms of stress are trying to tell you something. What's the stress? What's the change that's needed? The trick is to recognize stress as a signal and find ways to do things differently.

- **Expect to feel resistance.** The fact that change is inevitable doesn't mean you're going to like it. What if you aren't looking to make a change? Maybe you like the way things are now. You've always done things a certain way, and it's comfortable. Change introduces the uncertainty of trying something new. Anytime you're unsure about something new, you can expect resistance—from yourself and from those around you. To move through this resistance successfully, you'll need to accept that it's going to be uncomfortable and just allow yourself to be uncomfortable, even though it's difficult. Change is not easy. It's not comfortable at first but, in the final outcome, you'll be able to look at the changes you've made, see the positive results you've created, things you've done, and be proud of yourself and your family—rather than being stuck.

- **Take one step at a time.** Most changes don't happen overnight or as a result of one family meeting. It's important that you give yourself and others around you permission to go slowly, even though the temptation may be to leap ahead and get through the stress and pain quickly. Recognize that when you're in the middle of change, it is stressful and it's OK not to have it all together. Make one small change at a time, and take gradual steps forward. It's much more important that family members trust and support each other in making the change than just getting through it quickly.

- **Act in a new way.** One of the barriers to dealing with change is the tendency to do what you've always done. When you're in the middle of a life change, it's not unlike being in a foreign country where you don't speak the language. At first, you try to speak more clearly and a little bit louder, but the natives still cannot understand you. Sooner or later, you realize that you're not going to be able to communicate unless you do something differently.

- **Make new rules.** Each stage in the development of a family requires new rules. For example, when a teenager starts driving a car, new rules are needed regarding use of the car, curfew, finances, etc. Many families wait until their child turns sixteen and is about to get a license. Then, all of a sudden, they realize they face a whole new series of problems and that they haven't sat down and discussed or planned what rules are needed. When change occurs, new rules are needed to fit the new situation. In some cases, change may mean giving up some of the old rules. For instance, an older teen may get a job outside the home and, between school activities and the job, not have time to mow the lawn. Again, change creates the need for rules that fit the new circumstances.

- **Use outside help when you get stuck.** Families face many difficult life situations, and all families could use some support from other people from time to time. Periods of change are stressful and often create too much of a burden for one person or one family to carry. There are times when you try everything and nothing seems to work, or you find it difficult to act in a new way. Whatever the reason, when you feel stuck and just don't have the resources in your immediate family, you need to consult with an adult outside the family to get help. Being able to recognize when you need help and having others you can go to for help is essential.

Traps

- **Getting overwhelmed and stuck.** When stresses get so great that you don't have enough energy left to work on problems with your family, it's time to get outside help.

- **Expecting change to come easy.** The first time you try something new, it can be awkward, embarrassing, or even frightening. Doing anything that's new takes practice. So there's always a little bit of chaos and crisis as you try out different ways of talking to each other or handling new situations. Once you've had a chance to "practice" your new behavior, or new rules, it will become second nature.

- **Assuming the worst.** Changes that are difficult and awkward are not necessarily bad. A retired man can learn to enjoy solitude; a divorced woman can gain confidence as a wage earner; or a teenager can gain her family's respect for her musical talents. These are all periods of growth that can be embraced with some sense of joy and enthusiasm—and a little less tension.

- **Abandonment.** Once you reach a crisis, several things can happen. You can stay where you are and just be stuck on the problem, or one of you can fade out, start drinking, using drugs, or walk away from the situation. Unfortunately, life issues don't go away that easily. If you walk away from a problem in one context, you're likely to re-encounter it in another.

CHAPTER 7

HOW YOUR FAMILY CAN PULL TOGETHER TO SOLVE PROBLEMS

EVERY FAMILY HAS ITS PROBLEMS. Problems begin as ordinary difficulties in life, but they can escalate into major incidents. One day your car breaks down on the freeway; your kid gets into trouble at school and they call you up and say, "we need to schedule a conference with you"; your husband comes in the door angry at you when you had hoped that he would be supportive because you're upset; you find yourself screaming at him because you don't know what else to do; and you think that if you don't get help, you're going to explode. These steps will help you solve your family problems:

- **Know when little problems have turned into big ones**
- **Work together**
- **Have a problem-solving plan**

KNOW WHEN LITTLE PROBLEMS HAVE TURNED INTO BIG ONES

Family life is like a series of highs and lows that can be seen as opportunities and challenges. Little problems crop up and you handle them, making changes and getting along. But sometimes, a major problem develops or those little problems seem to multiply until you're in the middle of a very difficult time. This can happen suddenly and noticeably, or it can occur so gradually that you don't realize it until you're stuck. It is important that you recognize when a situation has gone beyond your ability to handle it and be willing to say, "I'm stuck. I can't do this by myself."

Often problems come up when one person wants to make a change. It can be a change in how work is divided around the house, a change in the rules, or a change in plans. You already know from the couples' cycle that usually one person gets ahead of the other when it comes to making changes. A common one is when a wife, who has been the family's social director or on constant duty with the kids, now wants some time off. This usually shows up in a series of arguments or complaints that sound like "I'm tired of doing all the cooking around here. Why don't you take a turn cooking for a change?" Her husband may respond by hiding out at work, in the garage, or sitting in front of the TV. The tension builds. Other common problems that come up for families are getting homework or chores done. For kids, the issues may include getting something they really want, getting the rules changed, or getting someone to stop picking on them.

Stress Is a Signal

Anytime you have a problem that you don't know how to solve, you're likely to be under stress. The symptoms of stress are different for different people but some of the more common ones are; sleeplessness, feeling tired, headaches, gritting your teeth, eating more or less than usual, or being more irritable, talkative, or quiet than normal. If you're feeling stressed-out, recognize this as an important signal that you have a problem developing, even if you aren't exactly sure what the problem is. This means some change is needed. You don't necessarily have to change everything you're doing now, but, as discussed in the previous chapter, you may have to add some new skills.

Stress itself is not the real danger. All families have stress. It becomes more serious when there's no one to share the burden; there aren't enough resources to balance off the stress. This is why it is so important for family members to share the burden and work together to fix the problems that are causing the stress.

Tips

- **Be aware of the signs of stress in your family.** Identify some of the symptoms you notice in yourself and your family when you are going through hard times:

1. _____

2. _____

3. _____

- **Stress is a signal for change.** This means your usual way of handling things isn't solving the problem, and it's time to do something differently.
- **Remember past successes when dealing with hard times.** It helps to remind yourself that you've been through hard times

in the past and have come through them, sometimes better off than before. Write down three problems that you and your family have solved successfully in the past.

1. _____

2. _____

3. _____

• **Admit it when you see that you're facing major problems.** The sooner you acknowledge there is a problem, the sooner you can begin to solve it.

Traps

• **Stopping normal routines.** A lot of times when people are stressed, they become immobilized and other responsibilities begin to pile up. They just sit there saying, "I'm not sure what to do," and get more and more bogged down, farther behind, and more stressed-out.

• **Catastrophizing.** Some people have a tendency to exaggerate their problems and shortcomings to the point where they feel like they're going to fall apart under any kind of stress. This makes it hard to think clearly, and turns what could be a manageable problem into a major crisis.

• **Ignoring the signs of stress.** Sometimes we think that if we go about our business and pretend the problem isn't there it will go away. It's more likely that the problem will just escalate. When you start to scream and yell at each other, that may be your cue that something's got to change.

• **Assuming that all stress is bad.** Even though it feels bad at the moment, stress may also be an opportunity to recognize that you have a problem so you can do something to get it fixed.

WORK TOGETHER

Family problems, and their solutions, almost always involve more than one family member. In most cases, if you could've solved the problem that's bothering you all by yourself, you would have already done it. Sometimes you just don't have all the answers, and you need the cooperation of other people. When you're facing a problem, you will still feel pressured. But if you can bring together a whole group—your family—and you can call upon all of their strengths, you can usually handle things a lot more easily.

Picture each of your family members as a twig. By itself, the twig is easily broken, but a bunch of twigs placed side by side cannot be easily broken. The same is true in families. The strength of each member is greatly increased by the support of other members. That added strength is the value of getting help from both family and friends.

For example:

> Your car is stranded on the freeway. As cars go by and nobody stops, you begin to get tense. You wonder if you're ever going to get help, and you're already late getting home. You think it through, and decide to walk to the next exit just ahead. There you find a telephone and call your wife. When she answers the phone, you immediately feel better because you're no longer alone and in a bad situation trying to figure out what to do. Finally, you get home. Your wife understands that you're still a little up tight, and suggests you take some time to unwind. You call a friend who knows a good mechanic and offers to help out. One of your kids has a friend who works in a used car lot. He says he can get you a loaner for a while if you need one. With all these people together, you're better able to solve the problem and let go of the stress.

Many people try to keep all their problems to themselves. You were probably taught that you're supposed to handle your own problems. If you try to figure things out on your own, you may end up feeling more and more frustrated. You can and do handle a lot of your problems on your own, but you can only take so much. Even strong people get overwhelmed. They begin to show signs of stress and break down in one way or another.

Men, in particular, tend to keep problems to themselves because they've grown up believing they're not supposed to express their emotions, and that showing their troubles or worries is a sign of weakness. They don't talk about things until they're really upset, and then they blow up.

When a man blows up, his partner tends to get quiet. And, in turn, her getting quiet provokes him to get even louder. This is a vicious cycle, and one that is not unusual for couples. Eventually, they get out of touch, and both begin to feel desperate and isolated. Now, the original problem is not their biggest problem. Now, their relationship is at risk. Their way of trying to fix their problem has become the problem. If your partner is one of those people who keeps everything inside, you should encourage him or her to tell you what is going on by active listening.

For example:

"You need to let me in on your troubles. Tell me what's going on."

"Just forget it. It's nothing."

"I'm worried because there seems to be something wrong, and I don't know what it is."

"Let it go."

"It would be nice to let things go, huh. I want you to tell me what's wrong so I can help. We can solve it together."

"I can handle it."
"You think you can handle it by yourself."

Working together to solve problems requires that each person carry their share of the burden. It is especially important for couples to know that both people will do what they agreed to do—that they will be there for one another. One way that people get out of balance is by developing a pattern where one person is always the helper and the other one is always helpless. The helpless person takes the position that, "I cannot do things for myself." The source of the helpless person's expertise is always someone else.

For example, a helpless person might say the following:

"What am I going to do? There's going to be so much trouble I don't know what to do. I can't tell you how upset I am. I've had a headache ever since I got up this morning."

"I see you're really nervous and upset about this."

"I can't help it. If you could just go alone, it would really help a lot. I'm so upset that I don't think I can handle this."

This is a hit-and-run approach to problem solving. She wants to give the problem to him and run. He needs to keep her involved in handling it because if he takes all of the responsibility and handles the problem alone, what will happen the next time there's a problem? The best solution for him is to get involved and help her deal with the problem. For her, it's to include him in solving the problem, not turn it over to him.

"We can work it out together."
is a better way to approach this problem than:
"Here let me take care of that. I'll do it."

At first she may resist by claiming she can't do it. This implies there's nothing she can do, but that he can do it all. Gradually, if he does not reinforce or support her position, she will have to begin to think, plan, and organize so she can do her share. Learning to talk to others about your problems, and asking for help, doesn't mean that you can escape the job of fixing it.

Families face some very difficult situations at times. People have accidents, lose their jobs, lose their homes, and struggle with all kinds of setbacks and obstacles. But we find that the most difficult problems are the people problems, the problems people have getting along with each other while they try to face problems together. When you develop a stylized, routine, repetitive approach to the problem, instead of solving it, you have created a whole new problem. The real problem has become your style of communication. As we said earlier, it's not the stresses created by their problems that gives families the most trouble, it's not having the resources to deal with them.

Talk It Over

Everybody faces hard times, and it's easy to get all bound up in them. Sometimes it helps just to talk with someone else about your problems. You let go of some of the tension by talking to others and can actually think more clearly. Then possible solutions can start to come into focus.

The first people you need to talk to about your problems are your family members, including the kids. Since everyone in the family affects everyone else, your other family members will already know that something is wrong. It makes it easier on you, and on them, if you let them in on what is happening. Facing hard times together means that all family members stick together and contribute to solving family problems. In almost any problem situation, there's something that each person in the family can do to help.

Learn to Ask for Help

It's not easy to ask for help. Some people are so used to trying to "stand on their own two feet" that they just haven't learned how or when to ask others for help. Sometimes it seems like it would be easier to talk to a stranger about a problem than to tell a member of your own family. This can happen for a number of reasons. You may think you already know what they're going to say. Maybe you think your family members don't want to hear about your problem. Or you may believe that they won't respond the way you need them to, so that it's better to not raise the issue than risk disappointment.

The key to getting support from your family is to be willing to ask for help and to listen when someone else asks for help. This includes your children. Kids often have trouble asking their parents for help—just as parents have difficulty asking their children for help. For family members to be able to talk with one other and help each other with their problems, all members must practice being good listeners and good communicators of their own needs.

When you start looking at a problem, it's a bit like having tunnel vision. You only see a portion of what's going on and, perhaps, only one way to solve it. Involving others can help just because several points of view are better than one. When you can see more of the problem or more possible solutions, you have a better chance of solving the problem. Ask yourself "Who could help with this problem?" Then go to your partner, your kids, or to a close friend and tell them you want their help to get the problem solved. Here are some opening lines that will help you get others on your team.

You can tell a good friend: "I could sure use some help. I want my husband to do some of the cooking but I'm afraid if I bring it up again, we'll just get into a big fight."

You can tell your partner: "I'm feeling stuck. I really need some time off from cooking, and I need your help to figure out how to do it."

You can tell your kids and partner: "I need your help in figuring out how to take off some time from cooking so I can have some free time once or twice a week."

Know What You Want

The first step in asking for help with your problems is to know what you want. When you know what you want, you have a better chance of getting it. Problems can't be solved unless you can be clear about what you want in place of the problem. Like using a map to get somewhere, you need to start with where you are now, and determine where you want to go.

Start by thinking about what you really want instead of what you don't want, or are tired of, or want to have stopped. Is it that you don't want to cook anymore? Is it that you want your husband to do more for you? Is it that you want your kids to start helping out? Or is that you want some time for yourself?

The following table lists some typical problems people have—and what they want instead. Identify three problems—or issues that show signs of becoming bigger problems—that now face your family and list them. Then, for each problem, fill in what you would like to have instead. (It helps to describe what you want in specific terms, for example, a specific style of house in a certain location, or an exact amount of money, or a specific thing. Having a clear idea in your mind of what you want will help you determine how to get it, and also ensures that you'll know when you've got it.

PROBLEM	WHAT I WANT INSTEAD
Ex. I won't discuss my needs with my partner because she cries when we argue.	My partner and I will talk over our differences. I don't hold back what I am thinking or feeling or stop listening to my partner, even when she cries.
Ex. My child is cutting school.	My child attends school regularly.
Ex. I don't like it when my child is disrespectful.	I want my child to treat me with respect, which means that I will hear words like "thank you," "I appreciate that, Mom," and "good morning."
1. _____	
2. _____	
3. _____	

Say What You Want

The most common mistake people make in solving problems is approaching them based on what they don't want. Once you have identified what you want or where you want to be, practice saying it to yourself and to the people whose help you want to enlist in meeting your goal.

Here are a few examples of this kind of statement:

"I can keep talking even if my wife cries. I don't have to get quiet or yell."

"I want to let you know that from now on when we're talking, I will do my best to stay in the conversation and keep showing my feelings if you begin to cry."

Say what you want for yourself—and avoid criticizing or blaming your partner. This is not the time to complain that he or she is too argumentative, makes fun of your mother and father, or has bad breath. You want to establish a safe, non-threatening atmosphere where you can begin to work as a team. Provocative statements, regardless of how accurate they may be, will only undermine your goal of working out your problems. The key is to tell your partner what you want. Say what you think and feel about the problem, then expect to listen to your partner's ideas knowing that they may differ from yours.

This may sound simple, but in practice it is really tricky. What goes on in families can be akin to a full-scale war. People tend to hold on to a lot of things they've wanted to say but didn't, along with stored up anger and resentment. Then, when it comes time to have a friendly discussion about working together to solve a problem, they have their ammunition ready. If you need to make your point by beating up your partner verbally or emotionally, you'll lose the opportunity to work together with a teammate. You need to let go of past disappointments when you want to work together to get something solved. Stay focused on what you want and working together with your partner to solve problems.

Here's an example from a couple who have decided to work together:

"I'd like to talk with you a little bit about how I'm feeling, because every time something comes up with our kids at school, I feel responsible or guilty. I start feeling like I've done something wrong, and it gets in the way of my thinking clearly."

"I'm glad you told me that. I know what you mean. I get very nervous myself. That's why I was yelling at you when you came in the door. I'm not really mad at you. I'm just nervous."

"Well, that's good for me to know. I always figure you can handle it, and I'm the only one who gets panicky inside."

"I pretend that I'm calm."

"So you're not calm, and I don't feel that much in control."

"I guess that's right."

You can start to talk about the problem together in a way that's revealing about your position about the situation; and not blaming, but saying what's going on inside yourself. Learn to share your thoughts and feelings, honestly and openly. Being committed and able to maintain an emotionally authentic exchange sets the stage for solving problems.

When you start to talk about powerful emotions, you or your partner may begin to cry. It's okay to cry when you're talking about something emotional. That's just one of the ways you express your feelings. It's common for a man to think that when a woman cries, it's because he's done something to hurt her. In fact, she could be crying for a lot of different reasons. Maybe she's worried about being a good mother, or she's thinking about something sad that's happened to her. She may be angry. Some people even cry when they're happy.

Just remind yourself that the tears are okay, and that you can both keep talking. She can still think, even if she's crying, and can also say what she wants. And, so can you. Our advice for both of you is, "Don't use your tears, or your partner's, as an excuse to lose focus or to stop the discussion." You need to be clear on what your point of view is and stay with it.

For example:

"I would really like to talk about the children. I'm having lots of problems getting them to do their homework and trying to get them to do their chores around the house. I just can't take it anymore. I work all day. I can't keep on like this. I'm exhausted."

"It's okay, we'll talk about it later. I'll be back. I've got something to do out in the car."

(He starts walking away.)

"I want to talk about it now. It's not going to go away unless we talk about it."

"Talking about things isn't going to change anything!"

"I would like for you to talk with me anyway. Let's do it now."

"Okay."

"Thanks. It means a lot to me that you're willing to talk to me about this. I've been really upset with the kids and trying to get them to do their homework."

"It's okay. I'll take care of it. Don't worry."

"I think that we need to talk about how we can get them to be more responsible and take on their chores without me having to stay on top of them all the time. I need your help on this."

(She's in tears.)

"You're starting to cry."

"Yeah, I'm really upset about this. I'm glad you're willing to talk to me, because I think it's going to take both of us working together to really solve this problem."

"I have trouble talking with you when you're crying."

"I guess it makes you nervous, huh?"

"Yes, it does. I figure I've done something wrong, and I just want to get away."

(That's what she needs to hear. If he can tell her how he feels when she cries, they stand a much better chance of being able to deal with it. Although it's difficult for her, she needs to persist—to make sure he understands why she's crying, and how she wants him to respond).

"I understand how you feel. I'm not crying because of you. I'm just extremely tired, and I need your help."

"Look, I'll stay and talk with you about this if you just promise not to cry."

(She must focus on the fact that her husband has a difficult time when she cries. She doesn't want to have to stop crying. She needs him to learn to be tolerant of her tears. It's important for her to stay focused on her task even though she has strong feelings about it. The same reasoning would apply if he were raising his voice or otherwise expressing strong emotions. She would have to let him know how his actions made her feel, and he would need for her to stay with him, despite her response to way he expresses himself. Don't let strong emotions be an excuse for stopping the problem-solving discussion.)

"I'm just feeling grateful that you're willing to stay and talk. Thank you for that. I'm liable to cry, and I need you to be here."

Get What You Want

Getting what you want often depends upon your ability to gain the cooperation of those you need to help you. You'll need to put your skills of **speaking up**, **listening**, and **cooperating** into practice to get everyone on your team pulling together in the same direction. As we've said before, you can do a lot more working together with your family than you can working alone.

When you take the risk of letting others know what you want, they may really help, they may want you to be clearer on what you're thinking so they can help, or they might just feel blamed or dumped on and start to react. You need to talk it over to clear up any vagueness or miscommunication and find out what your team is thinking before you can move on to solving the problem. Say what you want for yourself, and then be prepared to listen. Remember that whomever you've asked for help may either need more information on the problem or they may resist what they see as an extra demand on them. This "dance" of talking and listening may take some time, until everyone is clear about the problem and calm enough to focus on helping you find a solution.

Here's an example of this kind of exchange:

> "I want to have one night off from cooking each week."
>
> "What do you mean? Now, you want me to do something else. Don't I do enough around here?"
>
> "You're feeling blamed and dumped on. After all, you do a lot around here."
>
> "That's right. I do."
>
> "Well, what I really want is to have one night off a week from the cooking."
>
> "So you want me to do it."
>
> "You think I want you to do the cooking. Actually, I want your help on how to figure this out."
>
> "So isn't this just another way to get me to do it?"
>
> "I'm hoping we can figure out together how to get it done, and that doesn't have to mean that you do it."

Tips

- **Stop and think about whom you might ask for help.** Start by talking to the people in your house and then reach out to family and friends outside your home. Be willing to bend a little. Let go of your pride and accept help when it's offered. By getting the help you need, you'll build a stronger base from which you can solve more difficult problems.

Name one problem facing you and your family now. Think about who has helped you in the past, and list those whose help you think you might need to help you solve this problem

_____

_____

_____

- **Commit yourself to making a change.** Usually, when problems come up, you can solve them and move on. But sometimes even your best efforts just don't seem to work. That's when you know it's time to try something new or different. This may mean talking more, speaking more directly, or even being quieter. Only you can decide if you'll take the time and energy necessary to tackle a problem, to stop procrastinating or avoiding it. If you commit yourself to changing the way you act, you're more likely to get the full cooperation of others.

- **Expect resistance to your problem-solving efforts.** Once you start to make changes, you can expect resistance from yourself and others. Change is a natural part of life, but so is wanting things to remain the same. Until you get used to doing things differently, your first temptation will be to try using your old ways to solve it. Similarly, when you make a change, your family will attempt to return to the way things have been done in the past. In the example that follows, the child has been running the home for a while. Naturally, when her parents started trying to turn that around, they got some resistance:

"Our daughter has been in charge, or at least our equal for some time, and we decided to change that. We started laying out clear rules about what we want her to do. She started throwing things and got worse at first. One day she broke a vase during a tantrum. We made her use her allowance to replace it. We stuck by our new rules and consistently enforced them. It was worth the effort. Now, things are a lot better."

- **When someone is talking with you about a problem, listen quietly until they're finished.** You can't work together as a team unless you accept input from others, and show them that you value their help.

- **Let the person know that you have heard him/her by repeating a summary of what you heard.** This is a good way to make sure that you really understand what they're saying.

- **With shy people, or touchy topics, be encouraging.** Try statements such as:

"This is hard to talk about. Thanks for making the effort."

"It helps me to understand why you've been so mad lately."

- **Ask if the other person wants your ideas before you offer any.** Some people resent getting advice about their problems. Asking their permission in advance makes this less likely. Remember, advice that was not asked for may be perceived as criticism.

Traps

- **Keeping quiet about your problem.** You may not be able to solve every problem you face on your own.

- **Telling long stories to explain your problem.** Most of the people you'd like to have help you won't have the patience for—or may not understand—the stories behind the problem.

- **Blaming.** Statements that place blame, like:

"This problem is all your fault."

can make it much more difficult to get others to cooperate with you in solving your problems. No one wants to be in the position of getting blamed if things don't work out.

- **Springing your problem suddenly on unsuspecting family and friends.** Be ready to spend time preparing them, answering their questions, and addressing their concerns.

- **Talking about your problems at social events.** It may seem easier to bring up difficult issues with strangers or casual acquaintances, but they can't help you solve the problem.

- **Asking for help, then not paying attention to advice.** Most family problems can only be solved through the cooperative efforts of family members. If you ignore their advice, it may be difficult to get them to continue to cooperate.

- **Complaining.** It is pretty easy to say "I'm upset" or "I want things to change" or "I don't want to do this anymore." This may be the first thing that comes to your mind, but it won't get you on the path to problem solving.

For example, statements like:

"You never help me with the cooking. I don't want to have to cook every meal. It's your turn to do some of the cooking around here."

aren't going to help you solve the problem.

- **Expecting others to automatically fix your problem after you've told them.** Sharing your problem with others isn't the same as turning it over to them. It's still *your* problem.

- **Trying to pry the person with the problem open like a clam by asking questions.** For example:

"Look, what is the matter with you? Something is, I know it is. Just talk to me, would you? Come on. I know what it is. It's because of that argument we had over dinner the other night. I know that's what you're thinking about, so you might as well just spit it out. I don't want you to stand there and just clam up, because if you do, how the heck are we going to work this out? What's going on? I bet you had a bad day. Is that it? Did something happen at work? Tell me! I want to know!"

- **Letting family members get away with communicating that there is a problem but not talking about it.** Hang in there and let them know that whatever it is, you can figure it out better together. To open the door so you can be a part of it, you may need to help them put the problem into words. For example, you can say:

"You need to let me in on your troubles. Tell me what's going on."

- **Offering solutions before you understand the problem.** You may be eager to help, but make sure you're solving the right problem, or you could generate considerable resentment.

- **Interrupting the person who is trying to ask for help.** Asking for help isn't easy—the person sharing the problem deserves careful and complete listening on your part.

- **Turning someone else's problem into one of your own.** It's typical for other issues to come up while you're trying solve a problem. When another family member brings up a problem, resist the temptation to bring up problems of your own. It will just upset them. Try:

"Let's talk about my problem now and agree to spend some time talking about your issue tonight."

Instead of:

"This is what you always do. You want to talk, but you never listen to what I have to say."

- **Avoiding asking for what you want because you're afraid of "starting a fight."** Sometimes, to get what you want, you have to be able to face the possibility of stirring things up. Families need to fight. It's essential to working out their differences. You're going to have differences, and frequently, people will feel passionately about the issues. If your family avoids fights, the little issues that bother you will build up until they become big problems. Follow the rules for fighting in the chapter on couples to work through these conflicts, so you and your family can get on with solving problems.

HAVE A PROBLEM-SOLVING PLAN

Having a specific plan or "recipe" for problem solving can turn it into a simple process in which all family members can participate. This kind of structure can help you work together more creatively to resolve problems and conflicts. Once you try this planned approach, you'll realize how many things you've ordinarily avoided or censored that would be better off out in the open so that you could work through them together. This structure will also help give your family more of a sense of control by giving everyone a chance to be heard and to get what they want.

Read the following family situation. The tips that follow will walk you through a step-by-step problem-solving plan to show you how you can apply it to a difficult family situation.

Jan is a divorced single mother working at a low-paying job. She has very little time to spend with her three children. She has one very close woman friend and no relatives in the area. Bob, her ex-husband, travels in his work. He sees the children about once a month and is not involved in parenting.

The children are Amy, twelve, who is confused and has been doing poorly in school. She's been cutting classes, and getting D's. Sandra, fifteen, has been spending a lot of time hanging out with her friends. Like her friends, Sandra has been doing okay in school and hasn't been in any trouble at home or school; Gary, seventeen, is an honor student who is not involved in any activities. He would like to go to college but knows that his family doesn't have much money and thinks he should help out.

When you come up against multiple problems as this family has, it is easy to feel overwhelmed. Often, family members will disagree on which is the most important problem.

Tips

- **State the problem.** Choose one problem to tackle. You're more likely to be successful if you agree to address one problem at a time. Each problem you solve makes the next one easier. For the family situation outlined above, we choose to solve the problem of Amy's school performance.
- **Write down the result you want.** For example: "Our goal is for Amy to get at least C's in all of her classes."
- **List many possible solutions.** Generate every solution you can and write out a list. Encourage creativity and allow no one to criticize any suggestion. Include every possible solution even if it seems funny or ridiculous. You're not necessarily going to follow every suggestion. You're brainstorming—trying to create as many possible solutions as you can. Sometimes silly suggestions can help people be more creative. Make sure that each family member contributes at least one solution so that they stay committed to the problem-solving process. You'll notice that with everyone's ideas combined, you'll have a much longer list than you would have been able to think of on your own. So, you've already expanded the number of possible solutions.
- **Review the list together.**

Possible Solutions for Amy's Family

1. Take Amy out of school.
2. Send her to live with her father.
3. Get her a tutor.
4. Set up a homework schedule.
5. Give her rewards for good grades.
6. Work with a school counselor to improve her attendance.

- **Have each person choose two solutions that they are willing to carry out.** Look at the list of possible solutions and do your own prioritizing. Pick the top two that will work for you and that you would be willing to carry out. Each person has only two votes and must choose two different solutions. Don't be concerned that you're going to be stuck with a solution for life. This plan will be reviewed later to see if it is working.

- **Decide together on one solution to implement.** Choose the solution that is the first or second choice for most of the family members involved. You'll usually find that you have at least one thing on the list that everyone can agree on. Several solutions may be combined to form a working solution. For example:

"We will work out a homework schedule with the school counselor and give Amy five dollars for every grade point increase on her next report card."

- **Carry out the plan.** A plan of action is crucial for handling all the little details that go into achieving your goal. Figure out the details of who is going to do what and get each person to commit to when they're going to do it. Give each person some task to do so that everyone is involved in the success of the plan.

For example:

- Amy will do homework daily from 3-5 P.M.
- Mother will review all homework.
- Amy will have her teacher sign off on all of her homework daily.
- Gary will help Amy with her studies for one half-hour each weekend.
- Sandra will give Amy privacy in their bedroom during Amy's study hours.

- **Meet to re-evaluate the plan.** Set a time to meet again to see how the plan is working. Your meeting can be a time for acknowledging how well your team is doing and making adjustments as needed. Is the plan going the way you hoped it would? Are you getting the results you wanted? If you aren't, do you have a backup plan? Keep in mind that your purpose is to discuss your progress and decide whether you want to do things differently, not to beat each other up about what's not working.

Here's an example of an plan for re-evaluation:

- Amy and her mother will meet Friday to discuss the time spent on homework, the comments from her teachers, and so forth.
- The whole family will meet in one week to evaluate how the plan is working, and each week thereafter until grades come out.

- **Get help outside the family if you need it.** If your plan isn't working, you may need to get outside help. Someone who's not stuck in the problem may be able to give you another point of view and will add to your list of possible solutions or work with you in some way to help you resolve it. Think about who might help. A counselor, teacher, friend, doctor, or consultant?

Traps

- **Trying to tackle too many problems at once.** There's a natural tendency to try to tackle as many problems as you can, as quickly as possible—especially once you've dealt with the first problem successfully. Address one problem at a time. Then take a break. If you face too many problems at once, your success rate is sure to go down.
- **Letting problem-solving meetings drag on and on.** Be sure to set a time limit so that you're only problem solving for

thirty minutes to an hour at a time. You don't want lengthy, unfocused sessions that everyone dreads.

• **Getting deeper and deeper into your problems.** Sometimes when others try to help, they get all wrapped up and involved in the problem. If your solutions aren't working, getting more people to apply them won't help—and will probably make things worse. As more and more time and energy gets sunk into the problem, you'll start to hear statements like:

"That kid has been a problem ever since he was born. He's just like you."

"If you didn't treat him that way, things would get better."

In a case, like this, you're probably better off going back to the brainstorming stage for some new ideas.

• **Resisting getting outside help when you need it.** It's a big jump for a lot of us to ask for help. We're taught to handle our own problems. We know that if our car breaks down, we go to a mechanic; if we have a plumbing problem, we call a plumber; if we need to move, we get a real estate agent. But when it comes to personal problems, we really resist getting outside help.

Remember that one of the most important contributions you can make to a problem-solving effort is to recognize when you're stuck and that it's time to look for outside help.

Now you're ready to do some problem solving on your own. We've provided a form that shows a problem-solving plan we like and highly recommend.

FORMAT FOR SOLVING FAMILY PROBLEMS

Every person and family has problems or disagreements. Healthy people and families find ways to solve problems. They use their skills to get what they want together. If you have gotten past the people problems—yelling, fighting, needing to win instead of cooperating—then this format for solving problems should help you. If you cannot do this job together it may be a sign that you need outside help.

1. Schedule a meeting: This should be for a specific time and place for thirty to sixty minutes.

   Meeting date _____ Time _____ Place_____

2. Agenda: Agree on one issue you want to solve.

   Issue or Problem: _____

   _____

3. Solutions: Include ideas from everyone. Don't criticize any suggestion. Just list them here.

Proposed Solutions

1. _____ 6. _____
2. _____ 7. _____
3. _____ 8. _____
4. _____ 9. _____
5. _____ 10. _____

4. Choose a Solution: Start by having each person choose two solutions they like the most from the list. Check to see if there is one solution each person has listed. Choose the one that has the most support and, remember, you will only use this solution for a trial period of time:

_____

5. Action plan: List specifically *what* will be done, by *whom*, and *when*. Be specific.

What	Who	When

6. Evaluation: Set a date, time, and place within the next two weeks to meet and review your progress using the solution you chose.
   a. If no change has occurred, go back through steps 3-5 and come up with a different solution.
   b. If the solution is working, thank each other for making it work.

INDEX

CONCLUSION

WE KNOW YOU HAVE HIGH EXPECTATIONS FOR YOURSELF AND YOUR FAMILY. We hope this book has helped you improve your skills and how you get along together as a family. We also hope you will share these ideas and skills with others.

Families face many pressures today, and young people need to stay connected to their parents more than ever. Kids who feel connected at home do better in school, get along better with friends, and are less likely to experiment with drugs, alcohol, and premature sex. The way to keep your family connected is to talk and listen to each other and spend more time together both working and having fun. Continue to tell each other what you want and need as individuals and family members. Have family meetings where you practice speaking up, listening, and cooperating to solve family problems. This is the way to "build something better" for your family.

Please let us know how this book has been helpful to you. You can reach us to give us feedback at our postal address, our e-mail address, or our web page. We look forward to hearing from you!

Family Wellness Associates
P.O. Box 66533
Scotts Valley, CA 95067-6533
e-mail: familywell@aol.com
website: http//www.familywellness.com